DOORS of LOVE & LIGHT

AURACLE

Doors of Love and Light Auracle: Energize Your Space Using Love and Light; A Supplemental expansion to the Doors of Love and Light Auracle Card Deck, sold separately.

Copyright 2020 © Rita Morgin

All rights reserved.
No part of this work may be used or reproduced, transmitted, stored or used in any form or by any means graphic, electronic, or mechanical, including but not limited to photocopying, recording, scanning, or digitizing; web distribution, information networks or information storage and retrieval systems, or in any manner whatsoever without prior written permission from the publisher.

This book is not intended as a substitute for the medical advice of a physician or qualified therapist. The reader should regularly consult a physician in matters relating to his/her health and particularly with respect to any symptoms that may require diagnosis or medical attention.

For permissions contact:

An Imprint for GracePoint Matrix Publishing, a Division of GracePoint Matrix, LLC

322 N Tejon St. #207
Colorado Springs CO 80903
Email: Admin@GracePointMatrix.com
SAN # 991-6032

ISBN (Print): 978-1-951694-03-6
ISBN (eBook): 978-1-951694-04-3

Cover by Melissa Williams Design
Interior Layout and Formatting by Melissa Williams Design

All Images © Rita Morgin

Books may be purchased for educational, business, or sales promotional use. For bulk order requests and price schedule contact: orders@gracepointpublishing.com

DOORS of LOVE & LIGHT

AURACLE

*Clear and Energize Your Spaces and Your Personal
Energy with these Messages of Love and Light*

Foreword by
Karen Curry Parker

Rita Morgin
Artist, Author, Land Healer

Contents

Acknowledgements	vii
Foreword	viii
Instructions	x
Introduction	xiv
The Cards	xvi

1. The Door to Self-Love	1
2. I Allow the Divine to Hold Me Gently as I Heal	2
3. Nurture	3
4. Growing Trust	4
5. Opening the Door to the Crossroads Chording	5
6. Seeding Love/Seed Magic	6
7. Open Heart	8
8. Receiving Abundance	10
9. Healing Temple	11
10. St. Germaine and the Violet Flame	14
11. Spinning Possibility	16
12. Spiral Nebula	17
13. Network of Sacred Gathering Spaces	18
14. Metatron's Cube Sacred Geometry Energy Wave	19
15. Double Triangle Healing Grid	20
16. Guardians Activated	21
17. Clear Vision All Paths	22
18. Quan Yin Compassion	24
19. Nothing is Lost to God	25
20. Goddess Circle Trifecta Moves into Clearing Mold and Depression	26
21. Harvesting Joy	27
22. Spiral Pearlescent Light Activation Seal of Solomon/Star of David	29
23. Allowing Dreams of What Heaven on Earth is to You	30
24. Claiming Heaven on Earth	31
25. Scout Team Out to Peace-Make and Request Permission to Bring Healing in this Way	32

26. Allowing Abundance in My Life	33
27. Saturating the Land with Loving Healing Golden Light	35
28. Golden Torus	36
29. Big Guns Bagua Clearing	37
30. Quiver Birds	41
31. Forgiveness: Allowing the Experience to End Without Trauma	43
32. Crystal Harmonizing Energy	45
33. Dragon Tree/Giraffe Has a Voice	46
34. Gift and Blessing for the Land	48
35. Untangling Threads and Laying Down Swords	50
36. Archangel Michael Clean and Clear All Energetic Debris as Serves Highest Good	51
37. Opening the Well of Creativity	52
38. Love, Light and Elevation	53
39. Gift and Blessing to Former Occupants of the Land	54
40. The Ferris Wheel of Love	55
41. Bouncer	56
42. Saturating the Light Grid with Gentle Transformation	57
43. Yarrow Dreams	58
44. Four Corners Grounding	59
45. Miracle Zone: Blessing the Waters of the Earth	61
46. Thumb Stones for Grounding	63
47. Opening the Door to Owl Conversations	64
48. Creating a New Normal	65
49. Blank Card	67
50. The Gift of Releasing	68
51. The Gift of Receiving	70
52. Joy Finder/Joy Bringer	71
53. Claiming Heaven on Earth Here and Now	73
54. Calm, Peaceful, Flowing Light	74
Extra Cards	**75**
55. I Am Not Broken	76
56. Breath of Heaven	77
57. Dragon OHM	78

58. The Flower of Life				80
59. I am Magick					82
60. Maple Tree Meditation			83

Glossary					87
Disclaimer					97

Acknowledgements

Thank you to Katie Christman for stepping in at the last moment and providing the quality images for the card artwork.

Thank you to Michelle Vandepas for patiently walking me through all that it is truly needed in publishing.

I have much gratitude to Camille Roman, Camille Fine Arts for helping me start this journey of taking this Doors of Love and Light Auracle Card Deck from an idea to reality. This deck can help everyday people access the wonderful energies I use for clearing and blessing the land, homes and bodies with ease. Camille Roman's artwork has inspired me to complete the meditations, art, and booklet quickly.

Great appreciation to Joanne Margalit for helping me complete and format the art and the Instructions to this Doors of Love and Light Deck with lovely rainbow watercolor washes.

Thanks to Evelyn Rodriguez for help proofreading/editing this manuscript in the Palo Alto Shut-Up and Write Meetup and Lynn Ehrhart for the final edit.

Blessings and thanks to every person and land for co-creating a clearing with me. Through your connection, I have learned much to bring to this deck.

Blessings and thanks to all my friends who have been willing to co-create and explore when I have a new technique to try.

Foreword

We are all intuitive.

But most of us have forgotten how to connect with our own inner wisdom—our natural ability to "know" what we need to know to propel our lives forward and to heal what we need to heal to create momentum.

In the 30 years that I've worked as a professional psychic medium, intuition coach and teacher, the biggest challenge that I have when I am working with people is to help them trust their own intuitive insights and to be able to hear their own inner truth.

There is a Jewish saying that says, "It's not the fish who discovered water." Often, we are so immersed in our intuitive ability, we can't "see" or "hear" it.

We are taught by media, Hollywood and books that being "psychic" is an external experience. We wait to see "dead people" or for angels to appear at the foot of our beds in the middle of the night. We think we need profound signs and wonders to point us in the direction we need to go.

In reality, your intuition is constant. We have inner hearing, gut feelings, senses that point the way, but our collective conditioning around "logic" and "reasoning" cause us to doubt our own wisdom. We ask ourselves how it is that we "know" what we know. We want the proof—reasoning and scientific evidence to validate our inner knowing.

Sometimes, if we're brave enough to share our hunches with others, we are laughed at or we let others talk us out of our knowing only to discover, in hindsight, that our gut or our hunch was right.

With the DOORS of LOVE & LIGHT AURACLE CARD DECK, Rita Morgin, gives you a powerful way to remember how to trust what you know, how to hear your own inner knowing and how to access the insight and wisdom you need to clear the path to your next right step.

With innovative card layouts that blend Feng shui and her knowledge of clearing the energy of the land, Rita teaches you exactly what you need to do the clear the energy around you.

Each card contains beautiful artwork, accompanied with information that stimulates powerful insights, deep contemplation and support you in being connected more deeply with the knowledge you already have in a tangible, practical and workable way.

You learn to hear your own wisdom, your own inner voice and to use the cards to tune in more to yourself and your Divine Connection to Source.

These powerful cards are an essential tool to help you increase your connection to your own intuitive wisdom, gain deeper clarity about your life circumstances and to learn to trust your own inner voice so that you can learn to trust yourself and know that you are always loved and supported in your life.

Karen Curry Parker

Instructions

For clearing yourself, your home, property, workspace, and ancestral connections/lineage:

FOR YOUR LAND

Create a four-card spread of the directions:

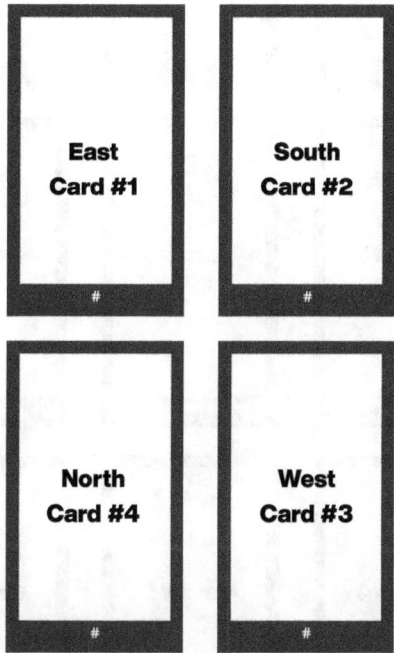

First card in the East, Second in the South, Third in the West, Fourth in the North.

These cards bring the needed energies to those areas of the property you are clearing. Look into those spaces to see the energy that the card chosen reveals.

FOR YOUR HOME

A nine-card spread for the areas of the bagua:

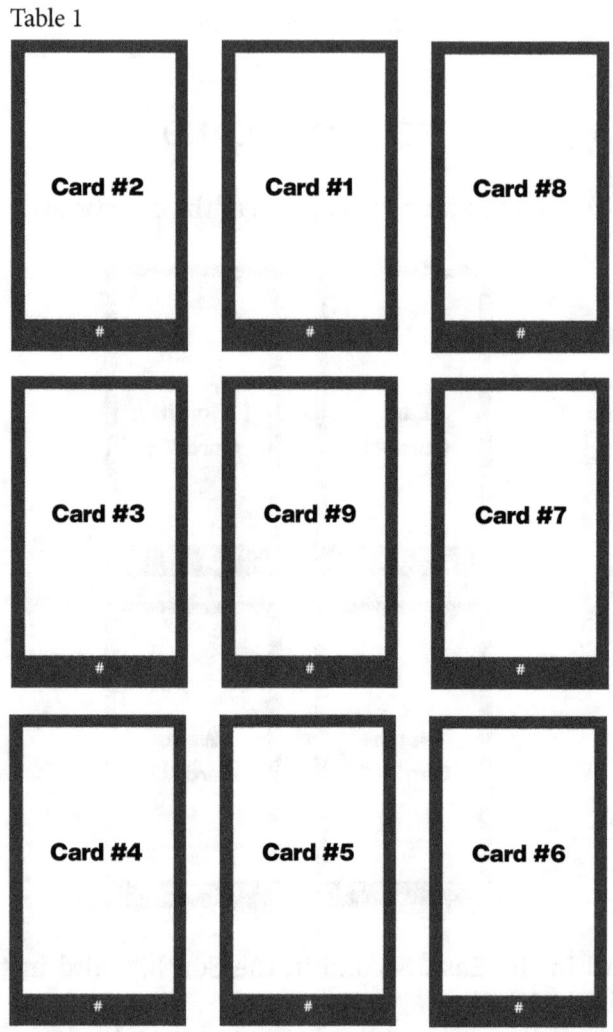

Table 1

Imagine your house is spread out like a Tic-Tac-Toe board. This is a specific drawing for clearing and balancing the energy in your house. When you care for the energy in your living space, you also care for the energy in your own body. This is the principle of "as within so without" and "as above so below".

To begin, CARD # 1, the card at the top Center is considered your front door and from there the rest of the cards are laid out. (See Table 1).

> CARD # 1 is your front door, the "Career and Mission" section of your *bagua*.
>
> CARD # 2 laid to the left of Card # 1, to the left of your front door (while you are sitting in the middle of your house), is the "Helping People and Travel" section.
>
> CARD # 3 is laid down below Card # 2; this is the "Children and Creativity" section of the *bagua*.
>
> CARD # 4 is laid below Card # 3; that is the "Relationship" section of the *bagua*.
>
> CARD # 5 is laid to the right of Card # 4. That is the part of the house that is farthest back from the front door and is called the "Vision, Fame, and Reputation" section of the bagua.
>
> CARD # 6 is placed to the right of Card #5; that is the "Money, Abundance" corner of the *bagua*.
>
> CARD # 7 is placed above Card # 6; that is the "Family and Ancestor" section of the *bagua*.
>
> CARD # 8 is placed above Card # 7 and to the right of Card #1. This is the "Knowledge Self-improvement" section of the *bagua*.
>
> CARD # 9 is placed in the center; it is the "Health Heart of Chi" section of the *bagua*.

As these cards relate to the space in your house, they also relate to a space in your body. I often get emotional tearful cards showing up in my "Health Heart of Chi" when I need to care for the energy in my heart and for my inner child. Often the clearing I do for my home affects me greatly and ends up being for myself.

FOR BOTH THE LAND AND YOURSELF

Rotating the Cards

As you explore your intuition, you will notice that sometimes you are drawn to rotating the cards. They look "prettier" or feel "right" when you rotate the direction.

This new orientation is a directional request from the land and your inner self.

Imagine around each card number, a compass rose with N, S, E and W (See Table 2).

When you find yourself drawn to view the card from a different perspective, the letter closest to the bottom of the card in this rotated perspective is asking for more of this flavor of "love and light".

For example, if you rotate CARD # 1 to the right, the east is asking for more Self-Love energy.

Table 2

Introduction

WHAT ARE DOORS OF LOVE AND LIGHT?

Bring the healing energy required to the spaces in need: in your home, your work, yourself and all the spaces of your ancestors...

Some *doors* invite you to clear your environment: the places you live and work, your ancestral lineage, and the spaces you travel through in your daily living.

Some *doors* invite you to journey inward to discover your whole being and the message of your heart.

Other *doors* (cards) invite you to care for both spaces at the same time.

This is not a future-telling Tarot deck.

This *Auracle* card deck provides an exploration in awakening your intuition. *"Auracle"* instead of "Oracle" because you are invited to see, hear, or feel the message of your own intuition and the aura (the energy around you), rather than be told what you need to know.

Each of us has intuitional access to all of the information in the universe. Support your journey to clearing, balancing, harmonizing, and energizing using your intuition in collaboration with The *Doors of Love and Light* Auracle Card Deck. Create your most joy-filled life.

I invite you to explore your understanding and appreciation of your intuition with my *Auracle* cards, meditations, and mp3s. Please use only what serves you and let the rest fall away. This book is only a tool to serve you in your journey to create and accept your personal knowing. If what I say is not your cup of tea, I invite you to utilize these cards to fine tune what is your "cuppa".

Blessings to all your days.

Rita Morgin

The Cards

These images are sacred geometries; I work with these two-dimensional representations of multidimensional flow of energy. I open up the coding in these two-dimensional forms to flow energy.

Cards one through sixteen are the beginning of the journey to create "safe and sacred space" for ourselves and our spaces. Cards seventeen through fifty-four begin a deeper journey into identifying, creating, and claiming your personal Heaven on Earth. Cards fifty-five through sixty provide the journey of closure so that we may open to the next chapter of our lives.

1. The Door to Self-Love

AN INWARD JOURNEY

Sometimes the greatest gift you can give yourself is love.
Where in your daily life do you need love and care for yourself?

Do you need to rest?

A day in nature? A cup of tea? A long bath? A good book?

Do you need to allow yourself to dream?

I invite you to explore and discover what heaven on earth would look like for you.

What would it look like to open that door of love for yourself?

2. I Allow the Divine to Hold Me Gently as I Heal

CREATING SAFE SPACE FOR YOURSELF

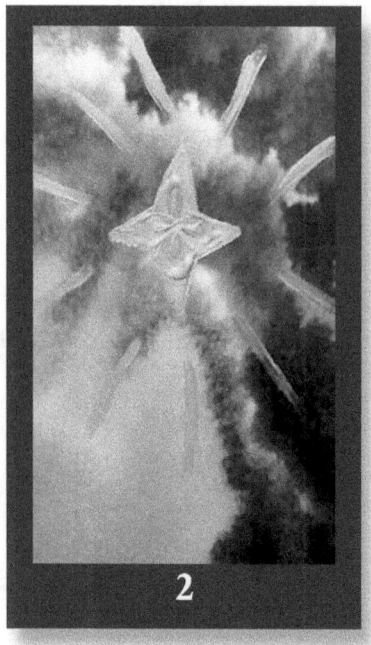

The open hands of the Divine are ready to hold your light gently, in just the way that is most comfortable for you. No pressure; no constraints... What is it you need from the universe to assist your healing journey?

Open the Door of Love and Light to support your healing journey in the manner that is most comfortable for you.

The most challenging part of my healing journey was in opening up to divine light and allowing it to hold me. My conditioning said that I could not trust the divine to hold me in a way I could be comfortable with. The invitation for me was to claim and conceive how I desired to be held and cared for.

3. Nurture

FOR BOTH YOURSELF AND THE LAND

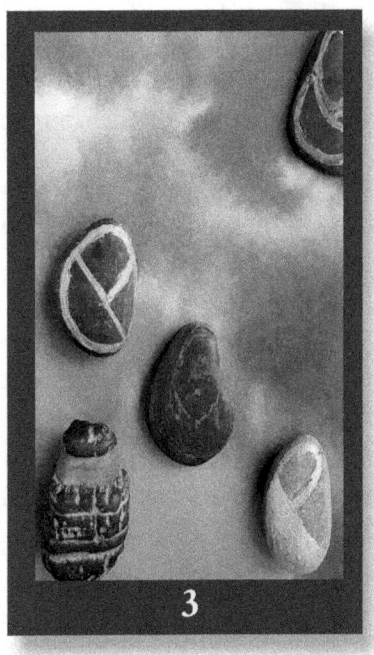

This Door of Receiving the Nurturing that you did not receive in childhood opens to bring love, light, and care to all those spaces that were told "No" and pushed away. This energy is often needed in the land, especially where there has been much abuse of the people and earth spirits.

Where do you feel this nurturing energy is needed to support you and your spaces?

What if the energy of need can be resolved right now?

I invite you to allow this blanket of rainbow light to comfort and support all of the spaces in need.

This is one of the three main doors that I open for almost every *LAND (LIght Aligned Nourishes Dreams) Healing* I do. The Land and the Ancestors also need this gentle nurturing light. Where in your space do you feel called to offer this light?

4. Growing Trust

FOR BOTH THE LAND AND YOURSELF

When I open doors of Love and Light, I state, "For all the spaces that have felt it was not safe to trust ... I am opening the door to Growing Trust."

This is the journey to find safe space in which to renew trust in one's self and the universe.

The Spirit of the Land supports you in this. She holds up a mirror of the abundance of life to reflect the abundant being you are.

What do you require to open your heart to the greening of your soul in this life?

What will nurture this growth?

Where in your spaces does the land require the energy of growing trust to replenish the life force in the land and your home?

Is it time to light up your spaces with the joy that you are and allow your spaces to do the same for you?

5. Opening the Door to the Crossroads Chording

FOR LAND IN TRANSITION AND YOURSELF

The sounds of the *Elements* surround you as you step forward into the crossroads of life.

Calling on the energy of "The Network of *Sacred Gathering Spaces* Across the Universe" to support your transformation as we open the door of love and light to The Crossroads Chording.

What line attracts your eye as you journey into your decision and discernment?

Listen to the song of your heart as you travel the lines of guidance from the Elements:

RED/ FIRE: *(Healing Haiku)* "The Light within, supersedes all other flames, all other magicks."

MIXED COLOR/ EARTH: *(Invocation)* "I grow my roots deep and deeper still. Greetings Earth Mother, I ask you to support my energy."

WHITE/ AIR: *(Invocation)* "I ask my divine guidance to assist my ears in hearing the truth of my soul."

BLUE-PURPLE/WATER: *(Healing Haiku)* Rain washes away, all that no longer serves me. I am wholly me."

6. Seeding Love/Seed Magic

FOR BOTH THE LAND AND YOURSELF

Opening the door to Seeding Love.

For all the spaces in need of love:

In what ways do we seed love in these spaces so that we may harvest love when it is ripe?

With this card, these possibilities are seeded in the land and nurtured with love and light.

This energy invites you to dream of what "harvesting love" means to you.

Saturating the land with golden healing light to nourish the seeds. Sprinkling the land with the silver tinkle of joyful dreams to enliven these seeds.

As the seeds grow, the words of nurturing form and take meaning. Look at the image.

Choose the words that are loving as you harvest the fruit...

FOR TRAUMATIZED LAND

Land that has experienced much transition, turmoil, or stagnation often needs an energy *activation* to flow vitality into the spaces. Then the property can be sold and the construction completed.

This card is often drawn for spaces that started construction and then were left abandoned or unfinished for years.

What are the blessings you desire to gift this land?

What are your dreams for this space?

What does the land desire and require to align with you in this dream?

Do you hear, feel or see the dreams of the land?

FOR YOURSELF

The Seeding Love card is often drawn after the end of a relationship or a period of personal stagnation.

Where has there been stagnation in your wellbeing?

What needs to be released for the soil to be fertile again?

... for your imagination to be enlivened?

... for your heart to heal?

Finally, what are the seeds you desire to plant and care for as you continue your journey through life? As you look at the image, what are the first words that come into your awareness?

Are these the seeds you desire to nurture?

Love? Joy? Companionship? Health?

What words come to you when you dream of what could be?

7. Open Heart

FOR YOURSELF

An Ocean of feeling opens my heart to the beauty of my being, the wonder of my space, and a love for all humanity.

Where do you need compassion to acknowledge your tears?

Where in your space do you feel the need to open your heart to the tears of the past?

When I draw this card, I state, "Tears flow through me for all the spaces grieving their losses and aloneness. Flowing waters of the ocean breathe and transform the flood of tears and sorrow into a flowing wave of compassion."

Open Heart Healing Haiku:

My Heart opens through
An ocean of feeling and
Beauty of Being

FOR THE LAND: AND SAFE TRAVELS

"Blessings to all the lands I travel through."

I often state this phase as I travel through places that have experienced trauma and tragedy.

I allow the divine light to open my heart and bring those blessings through my awareness and acknowledgement of those spaces.

Often the land, problems, ghosts and grouchy neighbors simply need acknowledgement in order to release the trauma held in the space.

When you walk through a space and suddenly feel dread or great sorrow, I invite you to offer blessings to the land and all of its former inhabitants. Now see if your energy improves.

8. Receiving Abundance

FOR YOURSELF

What shifts or changes need to be made in order to receive the abundance you desire?

What is blossoming all around you in preparation to receive?

Opening the Door to Receiving Abundance with clear discernment as to what blooms need Nurturing in order to receive.

For me, as I was creating my *LAND (LIght Aligned Nourishes Dreams) Healing* business, SpiritEarthMinistries.com, I suddenly realized that I had created no avenues for me to accept money; that day I created a PayPal account.

What energy do you require to receive abundance? This is the energy "Receiving Abundance" brings for you.

9. Healing Temple

FOR THE LAND AND YOURSELF

One of the spaces in the Land of the Golden Ray energy is a Healing Temple. This is *Sacred Space* where you can call in all the energies you require to support your healing journey.

What support do you and your land require right now?

In this space you may find your akashic records, the golden dragon that guards these spaces, healing chambers of rest, replenishment and renewal, gathering spaces for your spirit team, your ancestors, your past lives or the energies of your ancestors.

What are the energies that require realignment to aid your journey?

Rest here for a moment to receive the clarity and support that is here for you.

Transcript from the Land of the Golden Ray video:

The land of the golden ray is an energy that I work with frequently. When I am healing lands or calling in loving healing light to myself, I work with this golden ray energy. I feel I am a golden light streaming from the rainbow sky.

As I was first starting out in discovering my LAND Healing, I had a Spirit team that I called My Council of Elders; at some point the Council of Elders said, "You need a land on your Council of Elders since you are working with the land. The spirit of land needs to be represented here."

I said, "okay what land?"

"The land of the golden ray and that's all we're going to tell you; we're not going to tell you anything else." was the answer.

And I Ugh! At that time, I didn't know anything about the Rays, the golden ray, the great central sun, or all the ascended masters that are supposed to be from there. I had no idea I was already working with these energies.

I did know that I had Visions and Journeys into a land that was golden; it had several different Landscapes within the space, one of which was a healing temple. One space I now know is the Library people often access when they're doing akashic records work; one of the spaces is a great desert of Golden Light. There are many other spaces and energies including Godlike energy in this place, but I always thought of it as separate from the collective understanding and I just thought of it as visions and journeying.

I didn't think of it as a real actual place and so, when my counsel said, "Put the land of the golden ray on your Council of Elders", I freaked out and I said, "I will think about it." They wouldn't give me any more information.

Finally, I decided that I trusted my Council of Elders enough that I would put the land of the golden ray onto my spirit team, onto my Council of Elders. As soon as I said that, they said to look up the golden ray on Google. I did and suddenly understood why I work with this energy.

This energy (for me, and I honor that we each have different perceptions and experiences with energy) is a very gentle loving light. I use it to saturate the land and to create a gentle energy clearing. I use the thread of the golden ray to run a Figure 8 through my space, through the parts of the body in pain. I often bring that golden ray energy into my heart and just let it expand my heart. The golden ray energy helps open up my heart when I am grieving or when I refuse to honor the pain that I feel.

When I'm working with the land, it's a gentle energy that I can use to saturate the land, especially if there's been too much trauma or energetic distortion. Sometimes there's energetic faults in the land- like earthquake faults. Do you know how earthquakes create fault lines and fissures? Sometimes there are energetic faults in the land, and I use that golden ray to saturate that energy into the land. I specifically use that energy for the spaces where people trip up; sometimes there's a crack in the cement in that space sometimes there's no crack at all, but it feels like walking from one world to the next and you will notice people tripping over that space repeatedly. When I see that energy, I use the energy of the golden ray to saturate the land in that space, and then people stop tripping.

Hopefully this is a good explanation of the land of the golden ray and I invite you to explore the golden ray, the Great Central Sun, and other ascended masters associated with the golden ray, if you would like to continue learning.

10. St. Germaine and the Violet Flame

FOR YOURSELF, HOME AND THE LAND

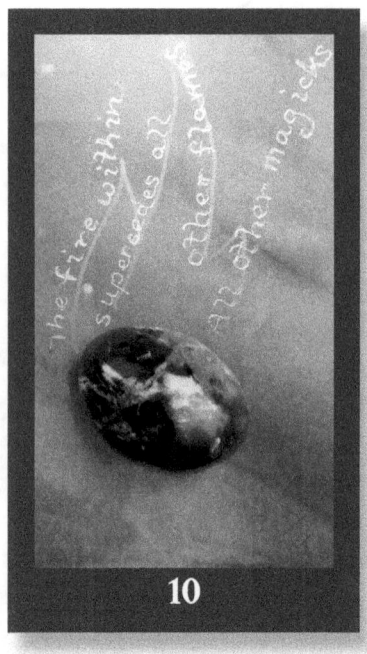

This is the card for: "I'm done with this nonsense!"

"Calling on St. Germaine and the Violet Flame to transmute all energies that no longer serve my highest good into loving healing light."

Clear. Align. Harmonize.

Where do you feel stuck energy in your body, your space and your productivity?

What needs to move, and yet, still seems stuck?

Is there clutter in your home that you just can't seem to clear?

Use the Violet Flame to shift the energy so that you are able to make progress more comfortably. I have added the violet flame energy to Metatron's Cube (card 14) and my Big Guns Bagua Clearing (card 29).

Big Guns Bagua Clearing Simpler meditation for those of us still in need of gentle healing light, like me, rather that deep shadow searching (A deeper questioning meditation is provided for Card #29):

Here's the energy for a Supercharged clearing with mugwort, frankincense, and camphor.

If you are able to sit in the center of your space facing the front doorway, imagine moving through the bagua (see glossary) using Archangel Metatron and the sacred geometry of Metatron's Cube with the added assistance of Saint Germaine and the Violet Flame. I invite you to Envision this Cube turning counterclockwise towards the left and slowly moving through your space. This is specifically a clearing to go through all areas of the bagua starting with the 'career and mission' area at your front door. Clearing the energy to light your way.

Then heading to the 'helpful people' section in a counterclockwise motion. Clearing the energy to allow the best people to help in the way you desire.

Turning left into the section of 'children, creativity and goals'. Calling on all the energies of Love & Light to clean and clear lighting up our creativity.

We're heading into the section of 'relationships, love and marriage'. Bringing loving healing light into all our relationships.

Turning left into the 'vision, fame and reputation' section of the bagua. Clearing the energy for our dreams to clarify.

Moving on to clearing the corner of 'abundance, money, and power'. Clearing blockages to receiving the abundance we require to thrive.

Turning left and moving into the 'family, community, and ancestor' section. Bringing loving healing light to all our ancestors and family.

Continuing, moving into the 'knowledge and self-improvement' section of the bagua. Energizing the discovery of self, honoring our well-being.

Returning once again to the 'career and mission', the energy now moves into the center of the space in the 'health, heart of chi'.

I invite you to allow this cleansing to continue moving energy to serve highest good, to clean and clear out all energies that no longer serve your highest good, to clean the spaces of the land: the air, the water, the metal, the Earth and the spirit.

Bring this energy to clear spaces that are really hard to clear, or clean. When you want to move forward, yet those energies are really stuck, it's a good time to call in the cleaning power of metatron's cube, Saint Germaine and the Violet Flame. With this energy, you can bring in the love and light and care that every being needs, requires, and deserves. All beings are held in love and light. All beings have the right to create Heaven on Earth Here and Now. You are welcomed to form relationships with your space.

When you need to get the energy moving to gain clarity, begin cleaning, or to move forward, this is a good energy to call on.

11. Spinning Possibility

FOR YOURSELF

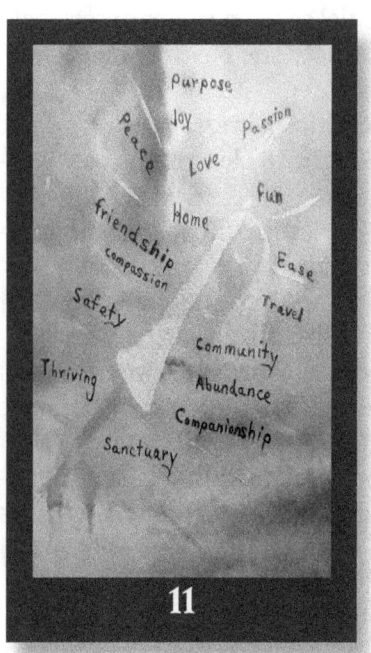

When I teach spinning wool to people at the fairs, they often ask me what I am doing. After the 100th time, I start saying "I am Spinning Possibilities".

With each choice we make, we are spinning possibilities for our future.

Take a moment now to explore the possibilities you desire to bring into this world.

Open the door, energizing these possibilities for yourself.

12. Spiral Nebula

FOR YOURSELF

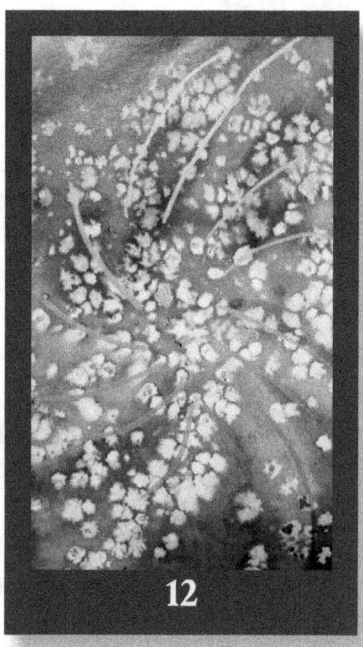

Everything in life is a spiral... the spiral nebula energy brings in the space for unwinding the tangles of living.

This cosmic energy invites you to sit back, relax, and allow the tangles to unwind themselves.

You are not required to do anything in this moment.

What music will add joy to your life in this moment and help you to relax and unwind here and now?

This is a 5-minute reboot break for yourself and the spaces around you.

13. Network of Sacred Gathering Spaces

FOR THE LAND AND MORE

"Calling on the Network of Sacred Gathering Spaces across the Universe to support this land, this body, and this moment as a sacred space of Love and Light to care for all energies in peace, safety and harmony.

No one may come into this space with harmful intent.

This is a place and a moment of healing. This space is held sacred throughout all time and space."

In my *LAND (LIght Aligned Nourishes Dreams) Healing* services at SpritEarthMinistries.com I re-dedicate and bless sacred spaces.

When this card is drawn, it asks you if a permanent dedication and connection with the Network of Sacred Gathering Spaces is advisable for this land, your mission, or your healing.

14. Metatron's Cube Sacred Geometry Energy Wave

FOR THE LAND

Your space is sufficiently upgraded to receive a quick healing "energy *activation*".

What would take 45 minutes in the "olden days" can be done in seconds to clean, clear, align and harmonize your space.

You are invited to focus on what you desire for this space to support and energize your wellbeing.

What does *Heaven on Earth* feel like for you in this space?

Activations tend to be a one-way flow of energy towards us. This activation is bringing in the energy you desire.

(My doorways flow energy both directions so that energy can leave or come whenever it is appropriate; i.e.: dead spirits leave to go to the next elevation; stuck energy flows outward, often escorted through the door, so that fresh energy may flow in.)

This Sacred Geometry Activation with Archangel Metatron includes: Flower of Life, Shri Yantra, Star of David, Golden Torus, Double Triangle Healing Grid, Four Corners Grounding, Saturating the Web of Life with the Golden Ray energy and many more.

15. Double Triangle Healing Grid

FOR YOUR SPACE AND THE LAND

This Double triangle healing grid is planted in the land for deep healing of trauma in the space.

It can also be called upon when the space is a place of healing to support the energy of all who are involved in the healing process.

Where are you looking at spaces in need of deep healing?

I often use this energy when I am in need of healing sleep for my body, when I am having trouble connecting to my strength, and when I am traveling through spaces which have a history of trauma.

This card is asking you to look at the places in need and allow the healing grid to saturate the space that comes into your awareness with this gentle healing light.

16. Guardians Activated

FOR THE LAND AND YOURSELF

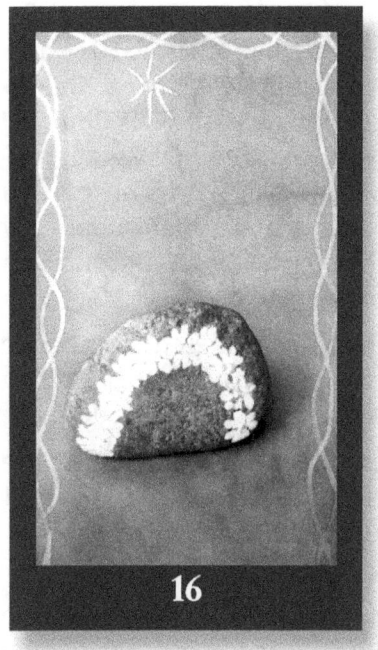

Each person and each space have spiritual guardians. It is time to activate them.

The guardians of your spaces are just waiting to align with you and your personal Heaven on Earth.

This card asks you to create relationship with these guardians so that you may rely on them and they may assist your "dreams come true".

What is the energy you desire to support you through each day?

Do you know what this energy feels like for you?

You are invited to:

Dream.

Create beauty.

Create community.

Create safety.

Shine the beautiful light that you are.

Give your guardians a job- an assignment to support your wellbeing and the wellbeing of your space.

Or simply enjoy the energy of the guardians activating.

17. Clear Vision All Paths

FOR YOURSELF

The image for this door is my one stone that has a name. His name is Ralph and he is my car Guardian. Ralph means "Wolf Council" in Nordic/ Scandinavian languages. A wolf will sit and observe all possibilities/ all angles and only speak up when it has information or warning to give.

I first encountered this door during my journey into becoming an artist creating "Faerie doors".

Lemon tree came to me with the energy of "clearing" so that I could "see clearly" the choices before me.

I then created a prayer stick to bring that energy instantaneously rather than traveling through the meditation.

My prayer sticks, like my rock doors, are the energy.

You open the door and step through; there is no long arduous journey required. We no longer need the trials and tribulations to discover our 'personal heaven on earth'. **This is the beginning of a deeper journey into the cards and yourself.**

When you are ready, the doors free the "instant knowing" that you have buried inside of your beingness. You know the answer best for you.

This door of Clear Vision All Paths holds the sacred space for you to explore the answers of your heart.

Lemon Tree Meditation transcript:

Lemon Tree brings a lot of clarity; just standing by the lemon tree, I get a breath of fresh air that calms me and energizes me at the same time. Some people wake up in the morning and drink some nice warm lemon water to start their day nice and clear.

When I'm with my friend lemon tree, I breathe in the scent of lemon's alignment and take a look at all the paths before me. For me, lemon tree is Heaven on Earth: clear and calm, peaceful and loving.

Lemon tree's meditation is "Clear Vision All Paths":

Lemon tree invites you to take a look at all the choices before you without judgment. See which things you like and which things you don't.

What inspires joy?

What inspires concern?

Look at those preferences to discover what best serves you and what doesn't.

Next, lemon tree invites you to sleep on it overnight; spend time with the land of the Golden Ray and Lemon Tree to gain clarity as you sleep.

When you wake up in the morning try a cup of warm lemon water and take a look at the possibilities/ choices again. Do they feel clearer? Which choice stands out as more joyful?

It may take several nights of resting with your desires to bring clarity to the choices before you, or it may be instantaneous. Sometimes waiting and dreaming with some choices, taking a look at it and then letting it sit for a while, resolves into clarity.

It's being pushed to make a decision now that creates the chaos and worry.

My friend lemon tree invites you to take the time to honor your awareness and inner clarity.

18. Quan Yin Compassion

FOR YOURSELF, HOME AND THE LAND

Flowing through the changes of life with grace and ease...

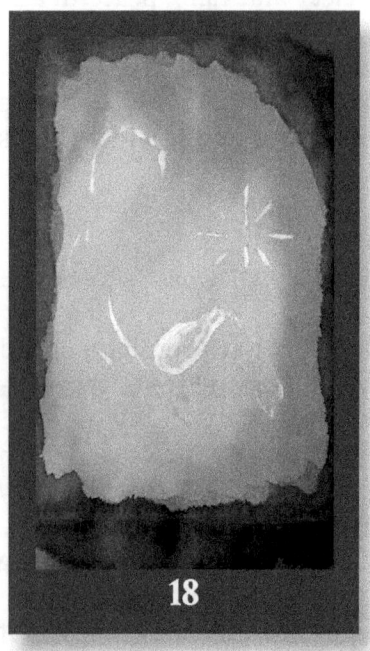

Quan Yin brings great gentleness and compassion to the spaces within you and your land that are greatly troubled.

When the pain is so great that you cannot bear to look at it, acknowledge it, or move beyond it, Quan Yin sits with you, asking nothing.

Nothing needs to be done in this space.

Gentle loving energy rests here with you and your spaces supporting your energy while you "grieve and process" in the way that is safest for you.

You are invited to take all the time you need here.

19. Nothing is Lost to God

FOR YOURSELF, HOME AND THE LAND'S LOST ANCESTORS

This is a finder card. When something has been lost, (whether it is a purse, a key, your way, unprocessed dead spirits or the spirit of the land) this card reminds you to:

Pause, connect with all of your beingness, and allow the divine to find it for you.

Sometimes, this means you turn around and find the key that you have been looking for during the last 20 minutes (exactly where you were looking).

Other times, unexpected things happen to resolve the energy around feeling lost and feeling something has been lost.

Most often, when I use this door, the chaos and fear of not finding the lost thing simply dissipates so that I can proceed calmly in the search.

What is missing in your life? I invite you to allow this energy in to support your search.

20. Goddess Circle Trifecta Moves into Clearing Mold and Depression

FOR YOURSELF, HOME AND THE LAND

This is a *sacred geometry* card that takes an ancient symbol and re-activates the symbol's flow of energy.

When mold grows, or when depression sinks in, the energy has become stagnant.

Each symbol you have ever seen is a representation of the ever-flowing energy that is life.

Allow this energy to move and flow through your spaces freshening the air, clearing the stagnant energy, and revitalizing your living.

21. Harvesting Joy

FOR YOURSELF

This card invites you to "Harvest Joy" right now.

Whenever we choose to experience joy in the present moment, we offer the opportunity to claim joy -

To our spaces,

To our companions,

To all who have come before us, and

To all who will come after us.

What brings you joy? What little things can you do right now to experience and share that personal joy with the space you are in?

Harvesting Joy meditation transcript:

What is it that you need to create your perfect heaven on Earth?

One of the ways that I help you create your perfect Heaven on Earth is by helping you open doors that you might not usually open. When I first started creating art, I started by painting doors (specifically Dragon-guarded faerie doors) using my dragon to make sure that it's a safe and secure space for you to bring up anything you need to look at and resolve.

I'd like to suggest opening the door of Harvesting Joy- a door that is always unlocked and it's always there for everyone, but sometimes it's the hardest door to open.

Some people have a misconception that you can't open a door to Joy and be joyous when other people around you are hurting. I have a different perspective. What if every time you open up a door to Joy you are adding a drop of Joy to the Community Joy bucket? And what if this makes it a little easier for everyone else to open this door?

When I painted Harvesting Joy, I gave myself an apple tree. On that apple tree, I have my favorite Apple; it is a mixture of yellow and green and red and it smells of roses with a slight floral smell. It's sweet, yes, but the most important thing in my Apple is this juicy tart tang.

I'm opening the door to Harvesting Joy.

What does your tree look like? What kind of fruit do you want to pick from your tree?

I'm picking my apple and I'm taking a bite and that sweet and tart, juicy, tang comes in and to me that Joy is dancing, and singing, and being out in my garden.

What brings you Joy; what can you do to Everyday to make sure you harvest joy?

What makes it so that you soar into the sky and at the same time you are so grounded well-into yourself, that no matter what is going on around you are home in yourself. You are fully embodied.

When I am dancing, and doing art, and gardening, and singing, I can be there with my friends. While they may not be joyful, I can still be there with them to support them without trying to fix them or shut them down. I do not need them to become joyful. I can allow them to be with what they are feeling. When they are ready, I am there to help them shift their energy. Harvesting my joy gives me greater patience and compassion for others, because I have greater compassion and presence for myself.

When I harvest Joy, I can allow you to be wherever you are and also be your friend. I am ready to lend a hand anytime you ask. To me, that's what harvesting Joy is.

What's harvesting joy to you?

22. Spiral Pearlescent Light Activation Seal of Solomon/Star of David

FOR YOUR HOME, LAND AND COMMUNITY

This is a moving, flowing sacred geometry activation for unwinding the tension and opening up the heart of the land, and then slowly saturating all of the spaces with gentle loving light.

This light gently emanates from the heart of your space, spreading love to your neighbors, your community, your country and throughout the world.

What beauty unfolds when we are able to saturate all spaces with loving, healing light?

From this space we allow the tension to unwind in its own timing. I invite you to rest here a few moments.

23. Allowing Dreams of What Heaven on Earth is to You

FOR YOURSELF AND ALL THAT YOU LOVE

When we experience a world of struggle, grief and desperation, it is sometimes difficult to conceive of what Heaven on Earth could be. It is easier to find fault and desire vengeance than to allow yourself to dream. So, we turn off the dreams and give up.

This card invites you to remember what it is to have dreams of: peace, love, safety, success, thriving, and joy.

The energy of this card is inspired by a quote from Marcel Proust: "If a little dreaming is dangerous, the cure is not to dream less ... But to dream all the time."

"Bringing in the energy to Allow Dreams of Heaven on Earth for your land, your home, your family and yourself."

What is the loving gift that you desire to bring to these spaces of your life?

24. Claiming Heaven on Earth

FOR YOURSELF

In this journey of "clearing all that you do not desire in your life, and your spaces" you are bringing a little more light into all the spaces you occupy.

This card invites you to claim the personal Heaven on Earth you have been creating.

When I open this door at the end of my second session in my comprehensive *LAND (LIght Aligned Nourishes Dreams) Healing* package, I say: "Spirit that I am, please flow through me your loving healing light to bring the perfect personal Heaven on Earth to each being and each place in this healing."

Are you ready to claim this Heaven on Earth for yourself?

Are you ready to request this for the lands you love?

Are you ready to allow each being to create this for themselves?

Each of these is a small step in creating Heaven on Earth.

"I acknowledge that your Heaven on Earth is not my Heaven on Earth. I allow you to create your personal Heaven on Earth, and I understand that your personal Heaven on Earth does not harm me in any way.

It is safe for me to claim my personal Heaven on Earth.

It is safe for me to allow you to claim Your Personal Heaven on Earth.

Thank you. Namaste. Rita"

25. Scout Team Out to Peace-Make and Request Permission to Bring Healing in this Way

FOR THE LAND

Before I bring healing energy into any space, I ask permission of the land, the ancestors connected to the land, and the current people residing on this land. It is as though I am sending a diplomatic party out to peace make before I even start the energy flow into a space, just like I would ask permission to touch you before I started a massage.

When you draw this card, I offer my scout team to assist you in requesting permission of the energies in need of healing.

The land is communicating with you.

How do you feel when you offer this healing to the land and your spaces?

What does the land need, to receive this healing energy?

What do you require to feel comfortable with healing your spaces?

The land is speaking to you now.

Sometimes, when the land has been traumatized with religious wars, the land itself will speak up and say how it wants to control the healing energy.

My scout team is here to 'peacemake' and heal those traumas.

Draw another card from the Doors of Love and Light deck: this is the energy the land is requesting from you.

26. Allowing Abundance in My Life

FOR YOURSELF

This card is here to remind you and your spaces that "receiving the abundance waiting for you" sometimes has several little steps.

1. **Dream.**
2. **Allow.**
3. **Receive.**

Sometimes our experiences give us a belief that it is not safe to allow abundance into our lives.

You have dreamed. And your hands are open to receive what you desire.

Now we open a door of love and light to care for the spaces in you and your land that don't feel safe to receive.

The energies of Quan Yin, Mother Mary, Mahatma Gandhi, the Land of the Golden Ray, the Web of Life, the Network of Sacred Gathering Spaces across the universe, crystal and color energies of turquoise, labradorite, fluorite, and magenta support all your spaces with gentle compassion.

In this sacred gathering space can you allow yourself to receive the abundance you desire?

When you choose to allow the universe and your spaces to support your dreams, abundance flows to you in unexpected ways.

Keep your hands and your eyes open to receive from these unexpected sources.

How much can you open your heart to receive in unexpected ways?

When I first opened this door, I did not realize how often I said, "No" to the ways in which I allowed myself to receive.

The first three steps in my healing journey were very challenging for me:

1. Choose the path. (It was so hard to admit that my healing journey was "opening up to spirit")

2. Ask for Help. (I was trained to never ask for help- that it meant I was worthless if I had to ask for help.)

3. Accept the help from wherever it comes. (Oh, it was so hard to receive help from people I had judged; And to release my expectations of help from those I had called friends.)

This card asks you to be patient with yourself.

You are moving into your abundance in the way that works best for you. No one else's path will suit you.

27. Saturating the Land with Loving Healing Golden Light

FOR THE LAND

A gentle, golden light saturates the light grid of the land and slowly expands into all of the property.

As the space becomes saturated, the golden light sinks down into all the spaces of the ground beneath the surface, gently relieving pressure in the fissures and other spaces of distortion in the land.

This gentle saturation is harmonizing the energy.

This card is drawn when the land needs extra gentle support, adding light slowly so as not to cause additional trauma.

28. Golden Torus

FOR YOURSELF, HOME AND THE LAND

The Golden Torus is a flowing fountain of life. It is the sacred geometry that is the mathematical basis for much of nature's creations.

Beginning in the heart of the land, and in the center of your space (Health Heart of Chi), a fountain of golden light rises up into the air and showers down in all directions.

This loving light flows deep into the earth and then rises up into the Health Heart of Chi (see Bagua). A continuous flow of this life-giving energy creates a sacred space of protection for you and your loved ones.

The land sings with joy when you choose to establish a connection with your spaces.

29. Big Guns Bagua Clearing

FOR YOURSELF, HOME AND THE LAND

This meditation is connected with card #10 and #14 using these energies together.

This bagua clearing uses the energies of camphor, California mugwort and frankincense together in an unusual combination. Separately they are very strong cleaning agents but together they create a beautiful *harmony* to add to this *Metatron's cube bagua* clearing. *Saint Germaine's Violet Flame* is used to burn up any energies that are blocking the flow of energy in your spaces.

Before you do house cleaning, use this Big Guns Bagua Clearing for the parts of your home where the clutter energy is very stuck or won't seem to move.

I did this recently for me because the "helpful people area" in my bagua collects clutter that I just can't seem to move and it's time to get it moving and let helpful people into my life.

If you have a specific place in your space that repeatedly collects clutter, it is time to look inward at where you are afraid to let the energy flow. The energy of this card and video supports sacred space for you to explore the need to use clutter to keep you safe.

Pull a second card for your land and run that energy on the land to move the energetic clutter of unforgiveness.

Simpler meditation for those of us still in need of gentle healing light, like me, rather that deep shadow searching:

Here's the energy for a Supercharged clearing with mugwort,

frankincense, and camphor.

If you are able to sit in the center of your space facing the front doorway, imagine moving through the bagua (see glossary) using Archangel Metatron and the sacred geometry of Metatron's Cube. I invite you to Envision this Cube turning counterclockwise towards the left and slowly moving through your space. This is specifically a clearing to go through all areas of the bagua starting with the 'career and mission' area at your front door. Clearing the energy to light your way.

Then heading to the 'helpful people' section in a counterclockwise motion. Clearing the energy to allow the best people to help in the way you desire.

Turning left into the section of 'children, creativity and goals'. Calling on all the energies of Love & Light to clean and clear lighting up our creativity.

We're heading into the section of 'relationships, love and marriage'. Bringing loving healing light into all our relationships.

Turning left into the 'vision, fame and reputation' section of the bagua. Clearing the energy for our dreams to clarify.

Moving on to clearing the corner of 'abundance, money, and power'. Clearing blockages to receiving the abundance we require to thrive.

Turning left and moving into the 'family, community, and ancestor' section. Bringing loving healing light to all our ancestors and family.

Continuing, moving into the 'knowledge and self-improvement' section of the bagua. Energizing the discovery of self, honoring our well-being.

Returning once again to the 'career and mission', the energy now moves into the center of the space in the 'health, heart of chi'.

I invite you to allow this cleansing to continue moving energy to serve highest good, to clean and clear out all energies that no longer serve your highest good, to clean the spaces of the land: the air, the water, the metal, the Earth and the spirit.

Bring this energy to clear spaces that are really hard to clear, or clean. When you want to move forward, yet those energies are really stuck, it's a good time to call in the cleaning power of metatron's cube. With this energy, you can bring in the love and light and care that every being needs, requires, and deserves. All beings are held in love and light. All beings have the right to create Heaven on Earth Here and Now. You are welcomed to form relationships with your space.

When you need to get the energy moving to gain clarity, begin cleaning, or to move forward, this is a good energy to call on.

Big Guns Bagua Clearing deeper meditation transcript: *Warning this is too deep for me! You may choose to explore the simpler meditation before you leap into this shadow-filled soul-searching journey.*

Here's the energy for a Supercharged clearing with mugwort, frankincense, and camphor.

If you are able, please sit in the center of your space facing the front doorway; imagine moving through the bagua (see glossary and Table 1) using Archangel Metatron and the sacred geometry of Metatron's Cube.

I invite you to envision this Cube turning counterclockwise towards the left and slowly moving through your space. (I first learnt this style of metatron cube bagua meditation from Deb Regan.) This is specifically a clearing to go through all areas of the bagua starting with the 'career and mission' area at your front door. What are the areas of my career that need illuminating? What is holding me back from stepping fully into my true career and life mission? Am I ready to allow this to clear today?

Then heading to the 'helpful people' section in a counterclockwise motion. Where am I afraid to let helpful people into my life?

Turning left into the section of 'children, creativity and goals'. Calling on all the energies of Love & Light to clean and clear. Where is my creativity stifled?

We're heading into the section of 'relationships, love and marriage'. What do I need to release in order to allow loving relationships into my life?

Turning left into the 'vision, fame and reputation' section of the bagua. What are the dreams that have been buried underneath the 'reality' of life?

Moving on to clearing the corner of 'abundance, money, and power'. In what ways am I blocking myself from allowing and receiving abundant living?

Turning left and moving into the 'family, community, and ancestors' section. Where is forgiveness required to release my ancestors of the projections of wrongdoing? How can I elevate my ancestors and family to be all that we truly are?

Continuing moving into the 'knowledge and self-improvement' section of the bagua. Where do I hide beneath the learning so that I do not have to step into truly being all of me?

Returning once again to the 'career and mission', the energy now moves into the center of the space in the 'health, heart of chi'. Creating clean and healthy space for my heart, my health, my energy.

I invite you to allow this cleansing to continue moving energy to serve highest good, to clean and clear out all energies that no longer serve highest good, to clean the spaces of the land, the air, the water, the metal, the Earth and the spirit.

Bring in this energy to clear spaces that are really hard to clear, or clean. When you want to move forward, yet those energies are really stuck, it's a good time to call in the cleaning power of metatron's cube.

With this energy, you can bring in the love and light and care that every being needs, requires, and deserves. All beings are held in love and light. All beings have the right to create heaven on Earth Here and Now. You are welcomed to form relationships with your space.

When you need to get the energy moving to gain Clarity, begin cleaning, or to move forward, this is a good energy to call on.

30. Quiver Birds

FOR YOURSELF

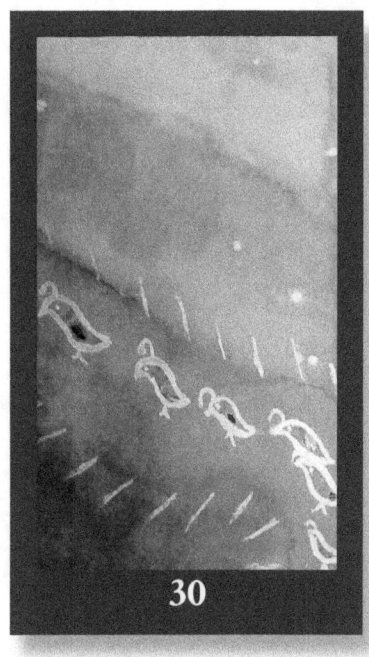

These gentle quail-like energies come together to support you in clearing your path so that the help and abundance you require have a direct line to you.

Call upon this energy when you have projects to complete, when you seem stuck in a lull and can't move forward.

The energy of this card invites you to pause, take a moment to realign with the purpose of the project, and allow a breath of clean air to energize you before you move forward.

One of the misunderstandings I had was that it was wrong for me to keep needing to realign my energy. I felt that I was wrong. I was useless. And I was broken, because I was affected by the energies around me. I was not good enough, because I needed to realign frequently. I felt that I could never win because I couldn't get with it and simply do as I was told. Whenever I did as I was told, I felt like I was dying inside; eventually that wrongness manifested as illness.

I did not have an understanding that this is the way we are programmed. When we are out of alignment, the "wrongness" shows up. The feeling of wrongness invites us to come back to our Center to balance and realign our energy.

What if there is no wrongness here? Perhaps the only question is: "what is your go-to for realigning?"

What is your go-to for reclaiming your integrity?

What is your go-to for restoring yourself?

Is there something that would energize you and help you realign to this "project" or intention?

For me it is a cup of tea with my sister.

What is your "go-to" for realigning?

31. Forgiveness: Allowing the Experience to End Without Trauma

FOR YOURSELF

Sometimes the challenge is letting go and allowing the experience to end. (For me this has always been my challenge.)

This card opens the door to forgiveness where the energy is clinging to the past with grief, fear and memories.

Are you experiencing a challenge moving through a time of transition?

This card is inviting you to free the space in transition with the energy of forgiveness.

"Opening the Door to Forgiveness:

Forgiveness for the spaces where you hang on . . .

Forgiveness for the need to leave a situation you had loved . . .

Forgiveness for any animosity still held . . .

Forgiveness for the spaces of shattered dreams."

What are the new dreams and experiences that you can invite to take up in this place of this release?

FOR THE LAND AND THE ANCESTORS

In the land, sometimes energies are stuck from betrayal, loss, and ostracization. And the ancestors have suffered greatly during these times.

For those energies, I invite you to bring in the energy of forgiveness so that they may be released to enjoy life again.

32. Crystal Harmonizing Energy

FOR YOURSELF, THE LAND AND THE ANCESTORS

"Calling in the crystalline energy of amethyst, clear quartz, black tourmaline, orange calcite, red jasper, violet flame agate, selenite and more to support you and your spaces."

Clearing and calming the agitation.

Aligning and balancing; receiving energy comfortably.

Energizing and Welcoming newly enlivened experiences of joyful living.

Supporting a "Miracles Happen" attitude.

33. Dragon Tree/ Giraffe Has a Voice

FOR YOURSELF, THE LAND AND THE ANCESTORS

Dragon Tree asks you to remember that spirit (your spirit) is willing to meet you wherever you are at.

You are not required to be different, improve, or change in any way. Your highest self-desires to support you, now.

"Supporting all the spaces in you and on your land that did not have a voice.

Blessing and healing all the spaces that could not find the safety and support.

Energizing the ability to speak up and ask for assistance, love, and compassion.

Supporting a gentle transformation into joy."

My story:

As I started opening up to spirit in my life, my meditation journeys were infiltrated by a dragon contorting itself into a tree so that I would pay attention to my spiritual needs.

Gardening was the only place in which I was willing to open up into my intuition. As I gardened, I would frequently see this blue dragon contorting and metamorphosing into a blue-green tree. It was hilarious watching this dragon struggle to become a tree. The Dragon Tree would then try to talk to me about opening up and allowing myself to heal. (Little did I understand that the dragon's contortions were mirroring my actions of trying to "do enough" rather than allowing myself to simply be.)

I would laugh and say, "You are not a tree!"

And then I could ignore the pleading call of my spirit, for I was not ready to hear myself speak.

Where is your spirit trying to get your attention?

Where are you being asked to open up to healing light?

Draw a second card for your land to bring healing energy to your spaces in support of this healing journey

More about my journey: "Blessings to you, Dragon Tree, you came to me when I was doing my best to be not spiritual, I was logical and surviving in this world without acknowledging spirit, and you were patiently there for me. Thank you."

As my friend, Dragon, came to me in daydreams and meditations, I painted him with Nettles from my garden. He was one of my first Faerie doors. A green dragon was sort of becoming blue in the face because he was trying to become something he wasn't, just to get my attention.

He wanted to show his love to me, even when I couldn't and wouldn't hear.

Dragon Tree's message was "I hold this space safe for you. I guard all the doors and I make certain no one is harmed in any way by them. All my doors are to bring love, light, joy, and elevation." This is how my dragon guards them. Anything 'other', such as pain or trauma, does not exist to my dragon. They cannot come in through the doors.

I wish to introduce you to my friend dragon who will guard the doors that I open for you and make sure your space is safe so that you can do, or see, or feel anything you need while you create your perfect personal Heaven on Earth.

Archangel Michael has assured me that Dragon energy and Angel energy do not conflict and come directly from Divine source light.

34. Gift and Blessing for the Land

FOR THE LAND

Are you in transition between living spaces? Reclaim your energy from former residences by clearing and blessing those lands.

Move into your new space with all of your energy in current time alignment. Are you ready to clear and release the trauma you have experienced in all of the places you have traveled through?

Whether we realize it or not, we leave energetic debris in all the places we travel through. Sometimes this energy is in the form of happiness, love, and joyful moments being experienced in that space. Other times it is great depression, fear, or Trauma.

Reclaiming your energy and clearing the energetic debris left by other people helps create a space that is in current time alignment which provides 'safe space' for the well-being of all people currently in it. Gift of blessing for the land is one way to create that Sacred Space.

Your gift can be a poem, a thank you note, a meal shared with your space, or an energetic clearing provided with these cards. What gift do you choose to bless the land with?

For myself, my journey into the gift and blessing of the land started with the fear of reliving trauma. I spent the weekend at an Enneagram Workshop learning how to communicate and facilitate communication between the different types on the Enneagram. I spent most of the time on the edge of reliving trauma and managed to still find a relatively safe place and not be re-traumatized.

Later, when I was working on the Doors of Love and light oracle card deck, I had a great awareness for card number 34 the gift and blessing for the land: "By clearing and blessing those lands move into your new space with all of your energy in current time alignment". Suddenly, I had the meditation:

Gift of blessing for the land Meditation transcript

By clearing and blessing all those lands you have ever traveled through, you may move into your new space with all of your energy in current time alignment.

You can do this with all the spaces you have ever lived in and bring all the energy of yourself back into your body in current time alignment. And it may just be as simple as that to clear the energetic trauma out of the body. This is what I did for myself; I do this process frequently as I encounter situations that trigger reaction from my traumatized inner child.

"Blessing all of the places I have ever traveled through, all the places I have ever lived, all of the places I have ever experienced anything.

Clearing those lands of all energies that do not serve highest good, most specifically trauma.

Reclaiming my portion of those Energies; cleaning and clearing that energy.

Realigning my energy to current time before my energy returns to my body.

To finish, I'm doing a full body reboot: reconnecting all of the meridians and reminding all of the lymph how to flow. Encouraging the lymph to clear out anything that's coming up and continue to flow life supporting energy throughout my body.

Thank you very much for joining me on this meditation journey.

35. Untangling Threads and Laying Down Swords

FOR YOURSELF, THE LAND AND ANCESTORS

This Door is peacemaking with all the places of conflict in the land. Many lands have had thousands of years of conflict, thousands of years with unresolved issues.

The peacemaking process begins with the laying down of swords... not only the physical weapons, but the words that attack, the isolation and silence that hides the truth, and the demeaning of value that makes "less than" of the "other".

Each energy coming into the pow-wow of "Laying Down of Swords" comes as equal. No one is left unheard and uncared for here. Each receives the energy that they require to allow the entanglement of the eons to unwind.

This is energy, unlike peace-talks, has no need for compromise. For with energy, all we need is the love and support that we were denied. "Sharing this supportive energy with all beings, all places, here and now."

36. Archangel Michael Clean and Clear All Energetic Debris as Serves Highest Good

FOR YOURSELF, THE LAND AND ANCESTORS

This is the Energy of Archangel Michael's Flaming Sword:

> The fire within
> Supersedes all other Flames
> All other Magicks.

This Healing Haiku claims sacred space for your wellbeing.

Your fire/ spirit is an essential part of living joyfully.

Heaven and Earth are supporting your light.

Will you allow your light to shine?

What do you need to "support your light"?

This energy is also used on land and buildings where energetic debris has been built up. It's like sweeping your home clean of all debris so that the light can fully shine.

37. Opening the Well of Creativity

FOR YOURSELF

In your Garden of Treasures, at the Roots of the Tree of Life, lies the Well of Creativity.

This well is always open to you.

What part of your life are you choosing to enliven with the energy of Creativity?

Healing Haiku:

Creativity.
In My Garden of Treasures,
The Well is My Source.

38. Love, Light and Elevation

FOR THE ANCESTORS

"Opening the door to Elevating the Ancestors. Elevating the dead who have not been cared for after they died."

When this card comes up, the land has unprocessed dead trapped in this realm. With the help of the Angels and/or the "Spirit of the Land", these people can now be cared for in the way of their understanding. Sometimes when people have traveled far from home, their families do not know of their deaths and there is no one to sing prayers for them to send them on their way. This energy door cares for all the spaces where tragedy falls and no one can assist the dead.

In these situations, the "Spirit of the Land" does it's best to care for these spirits until they can be cared for, but this is not the ideal plan. Those of us sensitive to the dead spirits are often their only hope of release. I created this card so that other people would not be freaked-out like me when I first encountered unprocessed dead speaking directly to me. I now have a spirit team in place ready to care for the dead spirits with this door. All I do when I feel this energy shift (which often comes in waves of smell like cigarettes or roses, sirens going by or a vertigo as if I stepped between worlds) is check that this is the door that is needed and assign Archangel Michael to do it for me.

39. Gift and Blessing to Former Occupants of the Land

FOR YOURSELF, THE LAND AND THE ANCESTORS

When a land is unsettled because of war, or loss of the indigenous peoples who had intimate understanding with the land, the land grieves with the humans.

Here we stand with the land and honor her grief by blessing and thanking the former occupants of the land.

You do not have to know them by name. And, if you do know the history of the land, this card invites you to thank them personally with song or poem or letter.

My letter to the Land and its former occupants:

I honor all those who have come before me in this space. I honor the land and the original peoples. I request permission to bring the healing energy to relieve you of your burdens and release you on to your next Journey. Blessings to you. I honor your journey through life. I honor your connection with the land. I am here to make connection with the land in this time, as you did in your time with this land. Thank you.

40. The Ferris Wheel of Love

FOR YOURSELF, THE LAND AND THE ANCESTORS

Love is a cycle like all things in life. Each goodbye opens the door for new love to enter. This energy cares for the emotions that haven't flowed during the circumstances of our beginnings and endings.

Where have you not allowed yourself to grieve? And how is this holding you back from opening your heart to love?

This card asks you to take a moment to honor those spaces of grief. I invite you to allow this energetic support to open your heart to the love that is looking for you.

41. Bouncer

FOR YOURSELF AND THE LAND

Here I share my Bouncer with you and your land: so that all energies brought up for clearing are processed with love in this sacred space of *LAND (LIght Aligned Nourishes Dreams)* Healing and not accidentally misdirected to others.

Imagine a big friendly orange bouncy yoga ball that guards your door, your land, your body. It joyfully bounces and then says, "Er!"

I laugh with joy when I see this image: Bounce... "Er!"

Nothing can harm me or my family when I allow this joyful light.

Where do you need to claim sacred space for your wellbeing?

42. Saturating the Light Grid with Gentle Transformation

FOR THE LAND AND YOURSELF

There are spaces in the land and our bodies that have experienced so much trauma that too much light, too fast, would cause blindness, earthquakes, or a collapse into fetal position.

While all my processes run on the principle that only as much light as creates gentle transformation will saturate the spaces, some lands request extra gentle saturation of these traumatic fissures.

It's like bathing the wound with honey rather than irrigating the wounds with water or scrubbing it clean with salt.

This door is acknowledging the trauma and the need for extra gentle care.

Where are you and your spaces asking for gentle transformation?

Perhaps you want to keep this card out for a couple of days to remind yourself of the need for slow healing and extra compassion and patience for yourself and your wellbeing right now.

43. Yarrow Dreams

INWARD JOURNEY

Yarrow is a very powerful medicine filled with courage, vibrancy, and clear boundaries. Yarrow Dreams open the door to creating and inspiring courageous dreams of joyful living.

One day, before I opened up to spirit, I had heard my *yarrow* plant request me to pick it and hang it up to dry. It was hung a good twenty feet from my bed around the corner of the room, and yet, this fragrance penetrated into my dreams with a colorfulness and vibrancy that disturbed my "sleep of ignorance" with inspired dreams of what would it be like if... I felt loved, I felt safe, I could be all of me.

Yarrow Dreams requests you invite this energy into these spaces of sorrow that cannot even conceive of Heaven on Earth Here and Now.

Where is your sorrow so great that you cannot feel a moment of joy? What if you can shift that energy in your dreams tonight?

44. Four Corners Grounding

FOR YOURSELF

Claim sacred space for yourself and your wellbeing no matter where you are. Allow others to claim sacred space for themselves.

When you are participating in events where you don't want to disturb the event and you want to be: safe, heard, and supported, claim sacred space for yourself.

I do this several times a day as I travel from place to place.

Are you ready to acknowledge your right to be here?

Here is a short meditation to teach this technique:

Claiming Sacred Space for yourself transcript (I learnt this Four Corners Grounding technique from my favorite energetic specialist, Lynn Ehrhart at Light Warrior Arts, lightwarriorbadass.com)

Four Corners Grounding is a simple technique. No matter where you are, you can claim sacred space for your comfort and wellbeing in seconds, aloud or silently:

If you're in a room, imagine drawing lines of energy on the ceiling from each of the four corners to the very center of the ceiling. Then, on the floor drawing lines from the four corners to the very center of the floor; now drop a line of energy from the center of the ceiling down through the center of the floor and deep into the center of the Earth. This creates energetic space for yourself and your well-being.

No matter what is going on around you, your energy will be cared for. For example, you're at a party and everybody is having a wild time but you're feeling kind of out of sorts, claiming space for yourself can allow everyone else to have an enjoyable time while you also care for your energy. If you're in a religious ceremony that has meaning and you don't want to interrupt the ceremony, but you find that your energy is not being cared for, claim sacred space for yourself. The energy of the ceremony continues to support the people who are being cared for during this ceremony, the energy is available to them in the way they desire it. And your energy is also being cared for in the way you desire. This is a way of quietly encouraging everybody else to care for themselves, allowing them to be chaotic if they want to be chaotic, and you are not harmed.

When you don't have four corners to mark, you can choose any four corners in your imagination. You don't need to know which direction your choosing either. If I'm outside, I imagine that I'm drawing lines from four corners that I choose about five feet above me. Then I imagine lines from the four corners on the ground I'm standing on. rather than drawing a line down the center of the room, I'm drawing the line through me from the center point five feet above me down though me and into the center of the Earth. "Greetings Earthmother, I ask you to help me claim sacred space for myself and my well-being."

I invite you to use this whenever you need, whenever you are traveling, whenever you're at home, whenever you suddenly notice that your energy feels off and you are quite sure why. This energy invites you to speak up for yourself and then ask yourself, "What is the most loving thing I can do right now to care for my body, to care for my well-being?" The answer might surprise you.

May you always know the beauty of enjoying Sacred Space for yourself.

45. Miracle Zone: Blessing the Waters of the Earth

FOR YOURSELF, THE EARTH AND THE WATERS OF THE WORLD

When Debra Halperin Poneman describes about being in the miracle zone, she talks about when one person is in the miracle zone then others can follow similar to a flock of geese.

Just before I heard this message, I Blessed a gallon of water with a full moon meditation and was inspired to share this blessing with the waters of the world. As I created this meditation video, a flock of geese flew right in front of me during the closing words. It felt as though the geese were taking the blessings with them as they traveled, helping to share the blessings.

Later that day, I heard Debra's meditation and a friend shared her revelation of geese as well.

These reflections of the geese in the miracle zone led to this card of sharing blessings to all the waters of the world. May you always be in the miracle zone!

Flowing Blessings to the Waters of the World meditation transcript:

Here I Am finding a river, a place where I can bless the Waters of the world. Here is the Palo Alto Baylands and this is the San Francisquito Creek. It is low tide and it smells very beautiful with the estuary stink of anaerobic bacteria. Sunrise shines on the water's path as it flows out into the San Francisco Bay.

I am pouring the water, sharing peace and love, joy and happiness into all of the places on this Earth.

Sharing Community. The water that I poured into the creek is trickling down to the outflow into the San Francisco Bay. Joining the larger body of water, the blessings are flowing out into the ocean.

Now joining all waters flowing into the cycle of water. I'm bringing blessings into each and every river; each river is bringing blessings to each and every land.

The blessings of the water are bringing in love, peace, joy, happiness, community, and healing, "May all places feel the love and the light. May all places share the Oneness of Heaven on Earth."

Here come the geese, three geese, to fly across my path claiming and sharing blessings of love to all the waters and all the lands they travel through, sharing a land healing blessing with you.

With which waters do you choose to share this blessing?

46. Thumb Stones for Grounding

FOR YOURSELF, THE LAND AND THE ANCESTORS

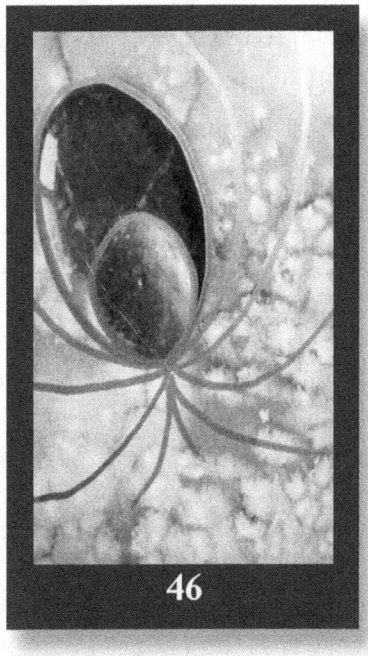

As I clear the land, I balance my energy before I try to clear any energy. Then I balance the land's energy.

Clearing unbalanced spaces disturbs the comfort level too much for creating a new normal of healthy energy.

I am often doing a balancing of energy first so that more light can bring lasting transformation.

I balance the energy in myself and then I share that harmony of balanced energy with the distress land.

There are three stages here: Clearing, Energizing, and finally, Welcoming. It can be challenging to clear before you balance, to energize before you clear, and to welcome all of you before all of the above.

I could not conceive of welcoming all of the darkness and the light with compassion for at least five years of "spiritual and energetic clearing" on my healing journey.

Where are you called to work on your personal balance? Feel free to chant the line of this mantra that resonates.

Figure Eight Harmonization Grounding Mantra:

1. Balance. Clear. Align. Harmonize.
2. Balance. Energize. Align. Harmonize.
3. Balance. Welcome. Align. Harmonize.

47. Opening the Door to Owl Conversations

A journey into the light. The perspective that owl brings is that we are all light and that nothing can truly harm us.

I fought this message so much when I heard it. My vision: "My dragon turned into 'Humpty Dumpty' and invited me to go on a 'Wild Light Ride' with him. As he bounced off the walls without breaking, he invited me to be wild-- for we were light and could not be harmed.

I felt like I was flying through a wormhole and when the trip was suddenly ended, I was dumped in front of Owl.

I watched Owl eat my children and then toss their bones up in an Owl pellet. I was suddenly faced with what I needed to release in the stories between me and my children in order to be the light that I AM and allow them to be their own light."

Owl asks, "Where do you need to release energy and become your light?"

48. Creating a New Normal

FOR YOURSELF

We no longer have a need to create painful experiences as normal. The universe invites you to create a "New Normal" with joy and ease.

What do you desire as your "new normal"? Where can you bring that "new normal" into your current life?

You are invited to take a moment to yourself.

As You create your "new normal", you may find it easier to choose that any pain you are experiencing is no longer your body's "normal" but only a temporary transition as you heal.

Use this card's energy, when you reach a point where you are forgetting how to connect to earth energy, when you feel like giving up because life's too hard, when you are in that transition between being in pain and creating health, and when you feel a healing crisis coming on.

We are now living in a world where we can make the changes we desire with greater ease.

Creating a New Normal energy transmission transcript:

This is a meditation I created to open up to a new way of being with my MotoKi Earth Energy Massage modality and 128 hertz music created specifically for me and my energy healing modality by John Bass Live.

When that space of awareness opens us up to realizing that chronic pain and adversity are not normal, it's an opportunity for us to create a new normal. It's an opportunity to not go back into the pattern that we've been stuck in for so long where our bodies think it's normal to live in pain.

This is an energy activation that you would use when you hit a rough spot and you just need a little help to create a new possibility in your body.

I have reached the point where I don't want any healing crisis. I'm no longer going to have a healing crisis and I'm going to allow my body's original blueprints (even though this body never got to utilize a healthy blueprint) to create a new normal of wellbeing in my body. It's time to create a healthy enlivened being without having to suffer trials or tribulations to prove I'm worthy to be.

I invite you to just get comfortable. Take some time to fall asleep after activating your new normal.

I start by leaning down into the energy, opening up to create the field I desire. What is the new normal you desire your body to experience?

This meditation uses Moto-Ki Earth Energy. Here we remind me your body that it knows how to energize itself with Earth energy.

Our bodies know how to bring up the energy we need to replenish and restore ourselves. We are reminding our bodies how to program the Earth energy we need to thrive.

Here we remind our bodies how to activate and move energy.

I am now running a reconnection circuit activating the blueprints for our original body that allows us to create that New Normal. I'm working on a blueprint that is how the human body was originally crafted to be, so that if you never had a body that functioned well, that new normal is still a potential in your field.

Charging up the lower Dantian. One way to recharge your battery to support this new normal is to put one hand on top of the other and then put your thumbs together creating a triangle with your hands and thumbs. Rest them in front of your belly button or on your lap below your belly button. You may activate this New Normal card to do this for you if you are unable.

Reminding your body how to create balance. Reminding your body how to choose balance.

Balance. Clear. Align. Harmonize.

Balance and energize all the lines of being.

I invite you to come back to the meditation whenever you have need to remind your body and your mind how to balance and create that New Normal.

49. Blank Card

FOR YOURSELF

What doors do you need to create for yourself?

It is time to do some soul searching with your dreams and desires. You are a great creator. Come and dream of the doors opening for you.

This is an angel card and they will stand by you as you are soul-searching.

If angels are not your cup of tea, here is sacred space for you to call in the energy you do desire to work with and allow it to support you.

I chose the number 49 for the doors you open for yourself, because it is a number of hope and trust. This number urges you to trust yourself and your capabilities. The number four is the number of foundation. Four is the Sacred Space on which to build. The number nine is the number of completion or endings; this journey of creating your own personal heaven on Earth comes to fruition in understanding which doors to open for yourself. When you draw this card your body, your space, and your inner knowing are saying that you know which door you need to open for yourself and your well-being.

May it be easy to do so; may it be joyful to open the door.

May you be blessed with all the wellbeing that you desire.

50. The Gift of Releasing

FOR YOURSELF

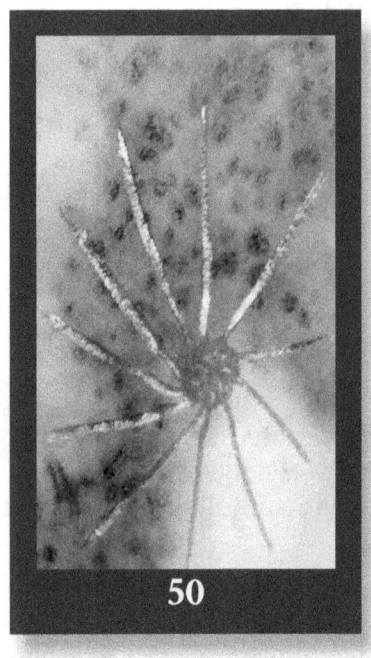

Reviewing my notes of the land blessings and energizing I have done in the past years at spiritearthministries.com, I came across a door I opened for a client called The Gift of Releasing.

This is a meditation for those moments where you find yourself with energetic debris that you've tried to release over and over again. You know that stuff doesn't serve your highest good. And you'd like it to go once and for all.

Open this gift and put in the box the debris that you no longer need in your life. Send it back to Source to be transmuted into the clean energy of possibilities.

And bring back what you need to create that beautiful future and that beautiful person that you desire to be.

Be that person you truly are.

What needs to be healed, released, balanced, aligned, harmonized, energized, and brought to my awareness for me to be the person I truly am? (A portion of this statement comes from the Quantum Alignment System EFT tapping sequence by Karen Curry Parker)

The Gift of Releasing meditation transcript

There are times in my life when I come up against old belief systems, and I go, "yeah it's time to let that go". Then there are times when it comes up and I release again and again and again; this door is useful during those times where my bias towards people repeatedly limit my enjoyment of life. I know that these biases do not serve my highest yet I seem unable to change them.

During these times, I invite you to ask, "what is the thing that I have been working on releasing and it's still not happening?"

For this meditation, I call forth the gift of releasing door and my spirit team guarding has Archangel Michael, Mother Mary, Quan Yin and Lakshmi.

This door presents itself as a present wrapped up with a big bow. I invite you to untie the bow, open the lid of the box and put all the biases and energetic garbage that you want to release into this box. Put in any little thing that comes up saying, "I don't need you anymore." or "I choose a more loving way"

I notice that the box is sprouting wings; it seems to start shining with white light and slowly flying up to the source of creation. I allow source to take all that energy back to the beginning of time. At the beginning of time, I call source energy "the roving at the beginning of time". This is the energy of possibility: energy hasn't been formed into anything yet.

I'm taking all those old biases and energetic debris that has been formed and I'm taking it back to a stage where it hasn't been formed yet.

I allow possibilities with dreams of how I desire to be to return to me. I bring that energy of possibility back into my field to help me to make my dreams a reality.

What dreams, what possibilities, do you choose to bring back to you?

I invite you to bring back your energy clean, clear and energized with source light now that you've released what didn't serve you.

51. The Gift of Receiving

FOR YOURSELF

"Bringing in loving healing light:

For all the spaces where we have distorted our understanding of receiving nourishment with the disconnect of anger and fear of power.

For those spaces feeling unsafe to create boundaries and feeling that change, power, wisdom, equals destruction and negativity instead of clearing and opening.

We bring in the energy for opening our hearts, minds, and hands to receiving."

This card is creating a space where it is safe to receive. "We are ready to receive. We are willing to receive. We able to receive."

My story: The gift of receiving has been my greatest challenge and learning experience. I could not create this card. I struggled for nearly a year contemplating this card. I finally realized that the energy in the Gift of Receiving was:

Allowing myself to reach out my hands

Allowing myself to be touched and receive.

I am starting with receiving the energy. Then receiving a dream of how I desire to receive. Of receiving Miracles where I least expect them. Of receiving kindness with Grace instead of shame.

Where does your journey to receive what you most desire begin?

52. Joy Finder/Joy Bringer

FOR YOURSELF

This is a Symbol creating session.

Would you like a quick connection with your personal heaven on Earth?

This symbol energizing and aligning is usually only offered with my comprehensive *LAND (Light Aligned Nourishes Dreams)* Healing package.

The land invites you to take the time to create and energize your symbol. Energize, amplify, and connect to your personal Heaven on Earth.

Let's shift the energy around your "problems" creating a different possibility.

This card activates the energy to connect and amplify your "joy finder" for you.

Once you feel connected to what brings you joy, you can amplify this feeling for yourself.

This symbol can be used to:

- Remind yourself what brings you joy.
- Energize your journey to creating your own Heaven on Earth here and now.
- Connect you with the north star to light your travels through life.
- Add a tool to your kit for discerning what choice serves you best.

Does this sound good for you?

What symbol reminds you to connect to your joy?

I invite you to draw that symbol now and activate it with drawing it, imagining it, or calling on it whenever you need.

53. Claiming Heaven on Earth Here and Now

FOR YOURSELF AND THE PLANET EARTH

Your land is ready to support you in creating sacred space for yourself and your wellbeing.

If you could have a space that felt like Heaven on Earth, what would that look like for you? When you come home at the end of the day, what do you want to feel? Welcomed? Safe? Comfortable?

What dreams and blessings do you have for the spaces you travel through: where you live, work, and play?

Please take a moment to realign to your personal Heaven on Earth by fine tuning your awareness of what brings you the greatest embodied joy.

54. Calm, Peaceful, Flowing Light

FOR YOURSELF

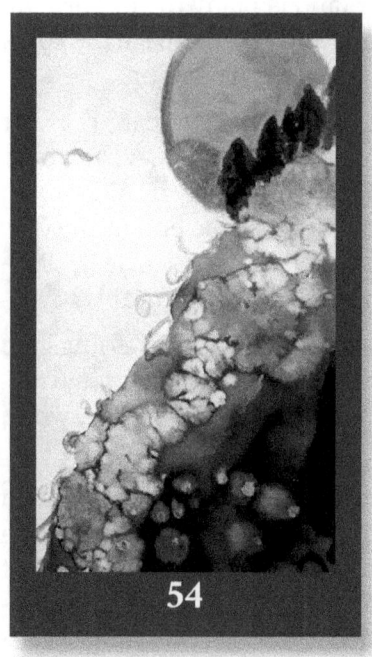

Healing Haiku:

Calm, Peaceful, Flowing.
Light Aligned Nourishing Dreams
Balance for my life.

This is the beauty of being in nature... of being a lover of nature. This card is flowing waterfall energy.

"Clearing away the chaos, bringing love and peace to the angry feelings.

Energizing the true being of you.

From this space of self-love, patience, and compassion, you are supported in looking deeply at your needs and gently claiming support from your spirit, the universe and the lands you live in."

Extra Cards

As I worked on completing this deck, recovering from a broken arm, and searching for a new home with like-minded community, some new cards appeared with the intention of acceptance, closure, and completion as I moved through these situations. I am adding these energies to the deck as an addendum to be used when closure is needed. They have not been not part of the deck for most of the times I have done LAND Clearings, but they May be meditated on, or added to the deck when there is a specific closure, a specific instance, or where you need to say goodbye and strengthen your inner being as you transition.

They are included in the following pages.

55. I Am Not Broken

FOR YOURSELF AND TRAUMATIZED LAND

"I am not broken." This was the statement I kept hearing from this lady statue with an injury to her arm. While we may experience trauma, we are not that trauma and it does not mean we are broken.

I am me no matter what I have been through.

And this was her message to me every day as I walked into the community garden. (She had been abandoned in the free pile). For eight months, I was unwilling to bring her into my community garden because I thought she was broken, because I was afraid, I was broken.

When I moved to my new home five years ago, I asked my housemates for permission to bring her in and fill her arm with shells from the ocean. She has found this place home ever since and wishes to stay when I move.

Many thanks to this land on which I have lived for the last five years. I have discovered that I am not broken.

And I have discovered many wonderful gifts that reside in me. These gifts help me to honor the spaces in need in all people and all lands.

All Thanks to the lady who insisted she was not broken.

This is a card for the land and yourself to heal Old Wounds and Trauma.

"Bringing in loving gentle light to honor the spaces that have been wounded.

Allowing a gentle light to bathe these wounds.

Bringing in the energy to heal, close the wound, create an ending, and discover completeness and wholeness."

56. Breath of Heaven

FOR YOURSELF

"I trust and allow your right to exist, your right to breathe, and I trust that your heaven on Earth causes me no harm."

I said this meditation to a yellow jacket who was in my way and trying to get my attention to tell me that a water pipe had broken on a property in which I was gardening. I have been allergic to bee and wasp stings previously, so stating this without fear showing up is a big deal.

Inspired by how well this worked for honoring all my feelings while staying present, I created a Breath of Heaven meditation. My plant friend, Breath of Heaven, reminds me that breathing is a part of creating Heaven on Earth. She encourages me to know that I have a right to breathe. I have a right to exist. And I have a right to be breathing comfortably for me.

It is your right to receive all that can assist you in mind, body, and soul.

Exhale and release all that no longer serves your highest good,

My friend, Breath of Heaven, says that you have a right to take a breath as easily and gently as serves you. There is no need to do it in a special way. Whichever way brings you closer to your Heaven on Earth is the way that's right for you.

Breath of Heaven says, "I honor your right to breathe. I honor your right to be. I honor your right to exist. I honor your right to create your perfect Heaven on Earth."

57. Dragon OHM

FOR YOURSELF AND LAND WITH UNBALANCED VORTEXES

This is the card that works on harmonizing energy in vortexes. Sometimes when your energy is being pulled off, it is not only cording between people, but this can be cording between vortexes present in the space in which you live and work.

In some ways your energy is a vortex, such as your golden Torus.

Here is an energy that can bring closure between you and any vortex; harmonize the energy in the vortex so that you are allowed to move forward.

This dragon OHM is a very deep vibration that can roll through your body like a waterfall. Sometimes it feels like a band of Taiko drums vibrating through the land and my body. Sometimes there is an energy shift, your mind releases and you're not quite sure that you really felt anything. This is a deep energy that rebalances all your cells and the energy on the land.

The energy of dragons welcomes you and your spaces. Sometimes there are vortexes in spaces that are not beneficial to human well-being. This card is drawn when there is vortex energy on the property disturbing the wellbeing of the inhabitants of the land. The dragons align and harmonize the energy for optimum wellbeing. Occasionally the vortex is a damaged connection between dimensional spaces; in this case, the vortex is closed and removed with the help of Archangel Michael.

A Light Dragon's Welcome:

I am Dragon.

I am the stars and the moon that light your way.

I am the air that whispers in your ears.

I am the path beneath your feet.

I am river of light that quenches your thirst.

I am the fire that lights all creativity

Come live and dance with me in the light.

58. The Flower of Life

FOR YOURSELF AND ALL LIFE

The Flower of Life is the ancient song of life and death that created time and space. The energy in the flower of life invites you to expand your connection within all parts of yourself, the earth, and the universe.

Where do you see your physical life represented in the spaces around you?

Where are you or your spaces feeling contracted, stagnant, and afraid of life?

The energy of the ancient song flows through all creation, expanding awareness, embodiment, and connection. Each verse is sung by the heavens during the journey of life.

Some of these verses of flowing life are Birthing, *The Greening*, Nurturing, Loving, War, Community, Grieving, Healing, Dying . . .

What do you choose to expand in this moment?

I see the Flower of Life opening my heart beyond my current awareness. In the image, I am embodied in the Golden Flower in the center; my awareness is the bronze outside of that Golden Flower. Beyond that is the next layer, the next awareness, of things that I barely know or connect with in this life. Beyond that is things I know nothing about. The Flower of Life is the connection between all things. And when I am fully aware, I realize that I am connected to all things and my awareness reaches beyond my body and what I know physically.

The Ancient Song by Rita Morgin 1998

Come to me my love. Come whisper on the Wind.

The wind brings your words to my ears,

Your kiss to my lips,

Your caress to my cheeks.

Spread across the universe we travel together on the Wind.

Sharing thoughts as thoughtless as can be

Spread upon the wind.

A zephyr brings music from the dawn of time to me.

The music travels everywhen, everywhere.

All that has happened,

All that will be,

Is whispered on the Wind.

A whisper touching my soul.

Our future, a whisper on our lips.

"Walk with me my love", calls a whisper on the Wind.

A voice calls to me, carried by the wind.

But the wind is the voice,

A lover from a faraway land, a distant ageless time.

Breathless as we sing and become

The Ancient Song.

Ancient words on the Wind of the Evening Sun,

Warming me,

A rod of energy

Spreading across the universe,

An ancient song bearing my name

Calling my heart

Calling me to act.

59. I am Magick

FOR YOURSELF

This card invites you to remind yourself of the magic that you are. Whenever you show the spark of Divine Light that you are, just being you and claiming your place on this planet, you help create Heaven on Earth.

This card reminds me to see what's divine in each person, but most especially myself.

No matter what's going on right now, no matter what appears to be taking over our lives, I choose to see the divine that you are. And I allow myself to see the Divine that I am.

If you look at the Masters who go through life 'enlightened', and you look in their eyes, you'll see that Divine spark of unconditional love, calm, and patience. This is because they can see the Divine that you truly are; they can see your true light instead of the chaos that we generally see around us.

Shine Your Light every day. The words "I Am Magic" inspire me to shine my light every day.

During the finishing of this deck, I experienced a broken arm, loss of housing, I gave most everything I own away and put the rest in storage, relied on the kindness of friends for a place to stay, and assisted my son who was experiencing loss of his housing as well. We filled out paperwork for housing together and prayed for assistance to afford the space as I had purchased the publishing of this deck and maxed out my credit... Still my world is blessed with magick.

What words inspire you?

What images inspire you to shine your light every moment?

60. Maple Tree Meditation

FOR YOURSELF

Rest, Replenish and Renew.

My dear friend maple tree's meditation came when I was doing a lot of pruning and Bonsai for the maple trees. Maple tree kept telling me to rest, replenish, and renew; and as I was doing this pruning, I was becoming more aware that maple tree knows exactly how to prune herself. Four to eight months out of the Year maple tree will go completely go dormant and rest; during that time, she goes inward and decides which branch is no longer serves and prunes them. Maple tree is a very smart; she goes through and prunes anything that no longer reaches the light, that no longer gives benefit to her growth. She carefully explores which branches best support her living and puts her energy there.

This is the message maple tree brought to me when I was ill in 2010 and had the beginnings of adrenal fatigue; at that time, I would try to meditate. Every time I would try to stop and just take a breath as my body started to calm down, I would literally be jumping up in fear and do something, anything just to keep moving.

Maple trees message is different: "There is a time to rest and replenish yourself; please take this time to rest and look within and see what no longer serves." Maple tree invites you to choose which issues to trim while you wait, and then move and grow in perfect timing. Like the maple trees in my area which grow from absolutely nothing on their branches to fully leafed out in less than 2 weeks, maple tree also knows "perfect timing". She rests; she replenishes;

and when the time is right, she renews her growth to branch out and spring forward with purpose, with life, with living.

This is the message I have come to appreciate with my friend maple tree. I now rest, replenish and renew my energy daily. I wait to move in right timing with the right people and situations as serves my highest good. I invite you to do so too. May your life be blessed with the synchronicity of perfect timing. Blessings and thanks.

This is the complete deck.

Thank you for using this deck to heal yourself and our planet.

Blessings to your day. From Rita Morgin at SpiritEarthMinistries.com

You can receive a list of live audio and video meditation links to many of these Doors of Love and Light meditations by joining my email list at SpiritEarthMinistries.com and requesting the live meditations pdf

Glossary

The Ancient Song—the ancient song of life and death that created time and space. The energy of the ancient song flows through all creation. Each verse is sung by the heavens during the journey of life. Some of these verses are Birthing, the *Greening*, Nurturing, War, Community, Grieving, Healing, Dying...

Archangels—Archangels are energies of light that have come to us from God (source) with much love, acceptance, understanding and deep compassion to help us. They will layout options for us to choose to provide the highest good – always making sure they obey the universal law of free will. They only want to empower you and will leave the choice up to you. They are never forceful or pushy, they always encourage and support us. Some like to laugh others seem serious. The main angels I work with are Archangel Michael and Archangel Metatron. I also call on the energy of Archangels Uriel, Raphael, Haniel and Jophiel. When I work with animal healers, I sometimes use Archangel Azrael caregiver to animals.

Archangel Haniel—Grace of God or the glory of GOD

Haniel is the caregiver to all nations. She empowers spiritual practitioners with the gift of heightened intuition, receptivity, self-awareness, self-compassion and self-acceptance as they open up to divine awareness. She is known for guiding those who seek to develop their psychic abilities, spiritual talents, and healing arts. Her energy is graceful, soothing, patient and welcoming.

Archangel Jophiel—Beauty of God.

Jophiel helps us when we feel insecure, cluttered, overwhelmed, and stuck. She honors the beauty in my soul, inspiring me to find the beauty within myself and my beingness. She helps me to express beauty from the heart of me and to see the beauty in others and my environment. I thank her for helping me to hold space and patience for where others are at. She helps me to appreciate and be grateful for the abundance I have, and to motivate myself to clear my physical clutter.

Her energy is warmly inspiring and energizing. When working with her I feel elegant. She reminds me of who I am inside, activating me to see a positive way through the clutter of my life.

Archangel Metatron—Highest of Angels

One of the two twins who were once human, but ascended into Angels, he works with me using sacred geometries.

He is often connected with Metatron's Cube, sacred geometries, the Book of Life which records everything that happens on earth, and 5D reality.

Because he was once human, he is more understanding of how humans work with one another and is extremely versatile with gentle clearing.

In this deck He helps clear, move and transmute energy.

Archangel Michael—He Who is Like God

I call His energy frequently, when it comes to spiritual protection and cleansings during my LAND (LIght Aligned Nourishes Dreams) Healing. He is a bodyguard, possessing great strength, power and courage. He has a flaming sword that can clear through to the truth of the matter where all parties/energies receive the help they need, clearing out any negative energies from our personal spaces of work and home.

His energy is masculine and grand, but when I am working together with him, I find his laughter helps breakup my seriousness and the fear that I might not be good enough.

He takes up a lot of space when he's around, so traumatized lands will not always accept his presence; at those times he steps back and I call forth other gentler energies from the understanding of the place am healing.

I call on his energy for protection when I'm feeling scared, exhausted, sense any dark energies, or would like him to clear my personal space or property, especially when I do not have the time to do it myself through meditation.

Archangel Raphael—God Heals

Raphael helps with healing on all planes (mental, emotional, physical, spiritual). I call on him to bring healing and safe space for children, pets and the land. His gentle green light helps support me as I heal past hurts. He assists those who heal others, such as doctors, nurses, and energy healers.

His energy is a loving, gentle green. He speaks with a soft compassion that brings comfort to heal wounds through all time. He is a great asset for generational healing to heal family dynamics emotionally, mentally, and physically. I use him to help heal generational trauma that oppresses many lands. One day when I am ready to go to South Africa, he will come with me to help heal my great uncle's past actions (1900-1930) in that land.

Archangel Uriel—the Face of God

The angel of wisdom. He gives people sparks of inspiration and motivation; I call on him to help me receive the information I require and let the rest flow past without wasting my time or energy on irrelevant information. You can count on Uriel to help shine the light of God's wisdom into your life, and as such I allow Uriel to guard my back.

Uriel can help direct your focus to receive the wisdom of God in your daily life. I call on him often, if I see my focus being diverted from the task at hand. He helps me to do "one thing at a time with all my heart".

Aura—the distinctive atmosphere or quality that seems to surround and be generated by a person, thing, or place. I consider the "atmosphere" is equal to "energy". When an atmosphere changes as you travel to a different place, it is possible that the aura of something in the new space is affecting your energy.

Auracle—is a play on words with a part of "auricle", the hearing bone, "aura" the energic spaces around your body and "oracle" the future teller of old Greece. "Auracle" instead of "Oracle" because you are invited to hear (auricle) your own intuition (aura), rather than be told (oracle) what you need to know.

Bagua—the 9 sections of the home in the Feng Shui energy map show which spaces of your building is corresponding to areas of your life. If your house is not a rectangle, the spaces of the bagua extend into your yard to create a rectangle. I use the Bagua as a basic structure for identifying energy stagnation in all buildings. See Instructions Table 1.

Balance—When the different elements of a space's energy are in the correct proportions it is easier to feel balanced, joyful, and in *harmony* with life.

Blanket of rainbow light—In card #3, the light of Nurturing comes in many different colors. You are invited to choose the form of nurturing that is right for you.

Energy comes in different flavors, colors, tones, feelings and forms of knowing. Each person has a specific frequency at which their intuition resonates fully. You are invited to explore what that is for you. If something doesn't work for you, it might simply be that it doesn't resonate at your optimum frequency. I invite you to take only what works, so you may feel happier, with more peace in your life.

Clearing—moves energy out. Whenever you move energy out, energy needs to be realigned and balanced to maintain the integrity of a space.

Crossroads Chording—The energy at the crossroads feels like a sound to me. As I explore the different possibilities, I hear different tones of energy. They feel like a cord or line of energy and they feel like a chord of music. When I feel harmony in this chord, I know it is the correct choice for me. My discernment is guided by the feeling I have for the sound of these energies: calm, peace and joy indicate alignment; fear, agitation and anger indicate energy in need of care to process; and tears, yawning, and burping indicate processing of energy.

Doors/ Doors of Love and Light—The cards and rock images that I have created are doors to open and bring energy in. They also allow energy to leave or transmute. This is different from an activation which brings energy in and a clearing which moves energy out. In order to have balance and harmony, energy flows both directions as is appropriate for the moment. All my doors are based on bringing Love and Light into the situation.

Dragon Tree—Dragon Tree is my personal symbol for my spirit calling for my attention. When I am unwilling to listen to my internal wisdom, I find this image of a dragon struggling to become a tree invades my awareness and alerts me to care for my well-being.

Earth Spirits—spirit or non-corporeal energies that belong with the land. There are energies that have never been human and are not from other places, planets, or dimensions. They are innately connected with the land providing for its wellbeing but they are not the land itself vs the Spirit of the Land which is the energy and sentience of the land itself.

Elements—The four Elements of earth, air, fire and water are used in the Crossroads Chording card.

Embodiment—The act of connecting your mental, emotional and spiritual awareness's within your physical body. In the 'olden days' people would ascend by transcending their bodies functions. Now we are being asked to embody our ascension through creating intimate awareness of our intuition and how it connects and intertwines with our physical body, spirit, mind and emotions. This book and deck's goal is to assist us in awakening this awareness of embodiment.

Another concept I bring to embodiment is that everything is inside you; you don't have to travel outside of your body to speak with your highest self or and other energy. It can all come to you with embodied awareness.

Golden Ray/ Land of the Golden Ray—The land of the golden ray is a very gentle loving light energy that I work with frequently. When I am healing lands or calling in loving healing light to myself, I work with this golden ray energy. I use it to saturate the land and to create a gentle energy clearing. I use the thread of the golden ray to run a Figure 8 through my space and through the parts of the body in pain. I invite you to explore the golden ray, the Great Central Sun, and other ascended masters associated with the golden ray.

Golden Torus—This energy circulates like a fountain gathering the energy at the feet, up the center of your body and out like a fountain. I particularly use this golden energy for clearing grief in the space of the heart.

Greening—When I work with trees and bring in the energy of possibility, I am "greening' with the tree. The energy flows up from the roots to the apex of the tree lighting up the nodes along the way, focusing energy at the spaces of new growth. This golden greenish energy spurs growth and new beginnings. I hear the verse of the ancient song that is "The Greening". There are many verses to this ancient song that permeates all creation. Healing is another verse of this ancient song and is only 2 notes different from The Greening. This energy flows up and out like a golden torus with a sheen of green added to it.

Harmony—When different elements of a space's energy are in the correct proportions, we create a situation in which people are peaceful and find ways to agree with each other. Now things seem right or suitable. As we create this harmony in the spaces, I hear a pleasant musical sound in the energy of a space as if it is made by different notes coming together in the same time. The harmony of a space occurs when all energies are given the love and light they require to thrive.

Healing—a verse of The Ancient Song is only 2 notes different from The Greening. The healing energy flows inward instead of outward like the greening. Instead of producing new growth, the Healing clears toxins and trauma, coats the spaces with loving healing light, and travels deep into the cells.

Heaven on Earth—We are the link between Heaven and Earth. Our bodies are created to bring the energy of heaven onto the earth, as well as bring the energy of earth into heaven. When working with Sacred Geometries, I become the conduit flowing these energies. All of us are this flowing conduit of Heaven on Earth.

Joy—is my north star. Joy is the sensation I feel when the land is cleared of energetic debris, then the land sings with relief. When a client fine tunes the energy for their wellbeing, joy zings through my body from head to toe.

LAND (LIght Aligned Nourishes Dreams) Healing— (Light Aligned Nourishes Dreams) Healing is the energy modality I created at SpiritEarthMinistries.com to provide energy clearing and blessing for the land.

Magick—a word-spelling variation of magic to indicate the energetic importance of ritual. Magicks have an energy charge that creates resonance, whereas magic is a trick of the eye or a deception.

Words are Magick. that is why I choose to use my words with care. When I find I have said or written something without care, I undo the energy I accidently put on the words and I re-energize the words with the appropriate energy I intended.

Mahatma Ghandi— from Wikipedia: was an Indian lawyer, anti-colonial nationalist, and political ethicist, who employed nonviolent resistance to lead the successful campaign for India's independence from British Rule, and in turn inspired movements for civil rights and freedom across the world.

Merkaba—from crystalinks.com:

"the divine light vehicle allegedly used by ascended masters to connect with and reach those in tune with the higher realms. 'Mer' means Light. 'Ka' means Spirit. 'Ba' means Body. Mer-Ka-Ba means the spirit/body surrounded by counter-rotating fields of light, (wheels within wheels), spirals of energy as in DNA, which transports spirit/body from one dimension to another."

I use a Merkaba the size of the planet earth when I do certain LAND (LIght Aligned Nourishes Dreams) Healing meditations.

Metatron (see Archangels)

Metatron's Cube—a sacred geometry symbol derived from the ancient structure of the Flower of Life using 13 circles.

From ka-gold-jewelry.com: "Metatron is in charge of all of creation and is considered an Archangel as well as a judge.

Since very ancient times, it has been believed that God created the entire cosmos according to a specific geometric plan. Sacred Geometry refers to the geometric shapes, patterns, frequencies, proportions, ratios, and laws that have been observed to underlie the organic life forms, objects and phenomenon occurring anywhere in the universe."

This is the most succinct explanation I have ever found to explain how and why I flow sacred geometry energy.

Mother Mary—In Christianity Mary is the Mother of Jesus. She is a symbol of mothering, nurturing and play. Her many names and symbols include Holy Mother of God, Queen of All Saints, Queen of Mercy, Queen of Peace, the mystic rose, the Fleur-de-lys. She represents our authentic humanity, encouraging us to fully embody our divine presence into human nature and our earthly experience.

Ogham—written alphabet of the ancient Irish language. Ogham or Ogam is an alphabet created with lines and slashes using the names of trees as the mnemonic to remember the letters.

To Peacemake—Diplomacy for energy left behind, abandoned during times of tragedy. In order to create peace, I send my scout team out to request permission to assist. There's No point in trying to heal if the energy is not ready or willing . . .

Quan Yin—Goddess of Compassion—one of the major deities in Buddhism and one of the most popular deities used in feng shui. Known as the Goddess of Mercy and Compassion, she is a great protector and benefactor, her heart is full of deep compassion and unconditional love; her energy is God-like: vast and patient.

Quiver Birds—a light energy with many changing forms including quail-like colorful birds that sweep my path clear for me so that I may travel freely and the help I need can easily reach me (they sleep in my quiver from a past life).

Sacred Geometries—ancient two-dimensional symbols such as the torus, Metatron's Cube, shri yantra, flower of life... represent multidimensional energy flow of creation. When these symbols are activated with energy healing, transformational shifts can occur. (see Metatron's cube)

Sacred Gathering Space—My mission is to recreate Sacred Gathering Space land by land, person by person, where each being can experience safe space to trust in and create their own personal Heaven on Earth Here and Now. These spaces are energetically connected and supported by a grid of light across the universe. We are protected by this network connection to create the atmosphere that serves the needs of those who feel called to work with the land in this place.

Sacred Space—A sacred space is a room, a house, or a location that feels like a sanctuary for anyone who visits. The goal is to make the person instantly feel a positive shift of energy as soon as they step into the space. For some, this feeling comes when they enter an ancient temple or a famous natural wonder; for others it may be a yoga studio or a meditation room. For me it is a garden. You do not have to go far to find a sacred space: you can create it virtually anywhere.

"A sacred space makes a person feel safe, grounded, welcomed, peaceful, inspired, and loved. It is a combination of physical items and people, but most importantly the intention that every detail of the space brings forth." (from spiritsciencecentral.com/create-sacred-space/)

Scout Team—I work with spiritual energies that serve me by acting as a scout (one sent to obtain information). I send this spiritual team out into the places I will serve to discuss what energy I am bringing to the space for the purpose of healing. I do this before the healing begins, requesting permission to touch the area of pain just as I would let a child know what I am doing before I help them.

Seal of Solomon—from Wikipedia: "the signet ring attributed to King Solomon in medieval Islamic tradition, later also in the Jewish Kabbalah and in Western occultism. It was often depicted in either a pentagram or hexagram shape; the latter also known as Shield of David or Star of David in Jewish tradition."

Source—the energy that created the universe, eternal love, God. Often called source light

Spiral Nebula—spiral shaped clouds in the night sky are galaxies lying outside our milky-way galaxy. Many things take form in a spiral: our galaxy, our DNA, snail shells, our plants all grow in a spiral pattern moving from the inside out in a rotating pattern. This is the creation energy I draw on to heal lands.

Spirit of the Land—Each place has a specific energy signature that resides in that space.

Star of David—A six-pointed star from ancient Israel, a sacred geometry symbol of flowing energy which I use in my LAND (LIght Aligned Nourishes Dreams) Healing.

St. Germaine and the Violet Flame—an Ascended Master, Saint Germaine is believed to have many magical powers including transmuting energy with the Violet Flame

Symbols—from Wikipedia: "A symbol is a mark, sign or word that indicates, signifies, or is understood as representing an idea, object, or relationship. Symbols allow people to go beyond what is known or seen by creating linkages between otherwise very different concepts and experiences."

I use sacred geometry symbols to access different types of energy flow. I see sacred geometries as two-dimensional symbols representing energy flow through multidimensional space.

The Ancient Song—the ancient song of life and death that created time and space. The energy of the ancient song flows through all creation. Each verse is sung by the heavens during the journey of life. Some of these verses are Birthing, the Greening, Nurturing, War, Community, Grieving, Healing, Dying . . .

The Violet Flame—a spiritual energy used to change negative energy into the gold of divine energy. The violet flame is from the violet ray, which has the qualities of mercy, forgiveness, freedom and transmutation.

The Tree of Life—in the Christian, Buddhist and Celtic writings the Tree of Life represents eternal life. The tree is believed to have healing properties and its fruit grants immortality. In Buddhism, the Bodhi-tree and is believed to be the Tree of Enlightenment. The Celtic Tree of Life knots represent the roots and branches of a tree woven together without end, showing the continuous cycle of life on earth.

Vortexes—a vortex is defined as a swirling mass of substance such as air, water, or fire.... Spiritual vortexes are said to be crosspoints between energy fields in the earth's grid system, or intersecting ley lines. (Taken from https://www.bemytravelmuse.com › energy-vortexes-around-the-world)   I feel that we humans are energy vortexes connecting heaven and earth.

The Web of Life—the structure that connects all living things. I see it as the energy through which all things are connected, not just the living.

The Well of Creativity—"Creativity is defined as the tendency to generate or recognize ideas, alternatives, or possibilities that may be useful in solving problems, communicating with others, and entertaining ourselves and others." (https://www.csun.edu/~vcpsy00h/creativity/define.htm)

I see creativity as a well of water at the base of the tree of life that is ever flowing and open to all of us.

Wild Light Ride—If you've ever ridden on Mr. Toad's Wild Ride at Disneyland, you know that you are jerked and bounced around like crazy. The Wild Light Ride is just like this only with a rollercoaster of light bouncing you off the sides of a wormhole.

Yarrow—Achillea millefolium, a flowering plant in the family Asteraceae known for its healing properties.

Disclaimer

I trust and have faith in your judgment of yourself, in your body and your spiritual well-being. If something on my website or publication is not your cup of tea, I trust you to honor your intuition and your faith in yourself.

Rita Morgin and Spirit Earth Ministries present the entire contents of this publication for educational purposes only. My goal is to offer you a different perspective and to allow you to create a different possibility in your life, thereby creating your New Normal and establishing your personal Heaven on Earth. This information is not intended to diagnose or prescribe for medical or psychological conditions, nor claim to prevent, treat, mitigate or cure such conditions. In presenting this information, no attempt is being made to provide diagnosis, care, treatment or rehabilitation of individuals or apply medical, mental, health or human development principles to provide diagnosing, treating, operating for any human disease, pain, injury, deformity or physical condition.

The information contained herein is not intended to replace a one-on-one relationship with a doctor or qualified HealthCare professionals. Any techniques Rita Morgin addresses only pertain to the underlying spiritual issues that may affect human well-being. Namaste.

www.ingramcontent.com/pod-product-compliance
Lightning Source LLC
LaVergne TN
LVHW051845080426
835512LV00018B/3073